Encountering God

Encountering God

AS A TRAVELING PAPAL
MISSIONARY OF MERCY

Father Jim Sichko

OPEN ROAD

INTEGRATED MEDIA

NEW YORK

ISBN: 978-1-5040-7320-2

Published in 2021 by Open Road Integrated Media, Inc.
180 Maiden Lane
New York, NY 10038
www.openroadmedia.com

This book is dedicated to my mom, dad, and siblings

"Jimmy is an only child that happens to have four siblings;
two older sisters and two older brothers."
—Bill Sichko, the eldest of Father Jim's siblings

Contents

Foreword

BY BISHOP JOHN STOWE, O.F.M., CONV.

As preparations were being made in late 2015 for Pope Francis's proclamation of a Year of Mercy, Father Jim Sichko, the priest of the Diocese of Lexington with the most frequent flyer miles, sent me a link to a description of the new office envisioned by Pope Francis: Missionary of Mercy. He wondered what I thought of this and whether I had designated someone for the Diocese of Lexington. By this time, I had come to realize that Pope Francis is always suggesting something new to bring attention to the ancient truths of the Gospel; he has been full of surprises ever since he appeared on the balcony as the new Bishop of Rome in 2013. His ministry as a universal shepherd has been marked by missionary outreach, an emphasis on mercy, and an insistence that the Roman Catholic Church go to the margins to discover Christ again. The idea of a

Missionary of Mercy made a lot of sense in light of the direction of the Francis papacy, and it ensured that the Year of Mercy would truly be experienced and felt throughout the church.

Shortly after seeing the link sent by Father Jim, I received formal notice that the Holy Father was expecting each diocesan bishop to name a Missionary of Mercy for our diocese. As I considered the description of the role and the importance of creativity in the exercise of this office, for which there was no precedent, I realized that it would coincide beautifully with the evangelizing preaching that Father Jim does throughout the country and across the globe. Father Jim seemed the obvious choice, and I happily nominated him for that role. I am grateful that Father Jim brings that designation to life and makes Christ's mercy real in countless situations in our diocese and beyond. He really does bring the role of Missionary of Mercy to life.

When Father Jim conducts a parish mission, usually called "Sixty Minutes for Jesus," I am inundated with emails from people who heard him preach at their parish on Sunday, were intrigued by what they heard, and came the next night and couldn't get enough of his message. Frequently, I hear that someone brought their skeptical teenager along and witnessed them come alive with interest in the faith. Many people who admit they had grown lukewarm in their faith share they were challenged by a story or even just a phrase they heard from Father Jim, and that reignited the spark of Jesus's Word in their hearts. It is also not uncommon that I hear from someone who is surprised by Father Jim's take on the Gospel and is curious enough to take another look, and yet another.

As powerful as the descriptions of the preaching encounters are, the yet more powerful stories are about the people Father Jim randomly calls on to answer a question. When the parishioner answers correctly, he gives away a take-home plant from the sanctuary (often to the pastor's chagrin) to help him illustrate a story. Time and again, it is the person whose special needs or difficult circumstances were unknown to Father Jim, but in God's providence, the participation and the attention from Father Jim were healing and supportive. Then there are the occasions when Father Jim is able to help someone bury a parent or child, to stretch their meager paycheck to include some urgent need, or when he challenges kids and adults alike to perform random acts of kindness, revealing the loving mercy of God to people who had given up on the goodness of humanity.

Father Jim is nothing if not creative with the role of Missionary of Mercy. Of course, he is eager to hear confessions, especially of those who have been alienated from the Catholic Church or have not availed themselves of the sacraments for long stretches of time. He is just as willing to hear the confessions of priests who are ministers of God's mercy themselves through the sacrament. But beyond the sacramental setting or the pulpit, he is also willing to be a minister of mercy in unlikely settings and unexpected circumstances: toward airline employees, restaurant personnel, law enforcement, random people in line at the grocery store, and the homeless in downtown Lexington. Father Jim elicits smiles at a time when too many are angry in their arguments and miss the bigger mystery of faith that while we were still sinners, Christ came to offer His life for us.

I hope you enjoy these stories of Father Jim's encounters and how he joyfully spreads the mercy of Christ. May you be challenged to be generous and may the smile elicited by these tales inspire you to make someone else smile today. Be an agent of the Good News—God is near, and God's love is unconditional.

Foreword

BY ED BASTIAN, CEO OF DELTA AIR LINES

More than two hundred million people fly on Delta every year. Among them is Father Jim, who flies regularly to destinations around the world for his life-changing work. He is unique among our customers, always looking for opportunities to inspire, reassure, and enlighten his fellow travelers as well as the Delta employees who are part of his journey. I often hear from customers and employees who have had the experience of sharing a flight with Father Jim and have witnessed firsthand the joy he brings to every moment, even when he's soaring through the skies at thirty thousand feet.

As a global airline, our mission is to bring people together and connect the world. It's hard to imagine anyone who embodies those values more than Father Jim. In a world that seems increasingly divided, he has the ability to unite people around simple acts of kindness, joy, gratitude, and warmth. He is a true practitioner of servant leadership in its purest form, and we can all learn from his example.

I'll close with some words of inspiration from Father Jim himself: "The only person you should try to be better than is the person you were yesterday." Through reading this book and learning from Father Jim, I'm sure we're better than we were yesterday.

As we like to say at Delta, Keep Climbing.

Growing Through Change

I'm the youngest of five children, raised in a Slovak/Italian Catholic family. I was born in Pittsburgh yet grew up in Orange, a small town in Southeast Texas. In the Sichko household, my parents taught us the importance of getting together for worship. I embraced that idea as a child and loved every moment of Mass. There was something special for me about the sense of togetherness we shared at church, which acted as our community and the heartbeat that bound us together.

Before entering the priesthood, I did my undergraduate studies at the New England Conservatory of Music in Vocal Performance and Opera. I loved singing. For a stint, I performed with the Boston Pops as a vocalist. It was a dream to sing and perform alongside such talented musicians, but still, I knew from a young age that I wanted to be a priest. Even as a child, while other kids played "policemen" or "baseball player" and other make-believe games, I was always the kid who played "priest."

Seriously—no kidding.

I loved the smell of incense on holy days. I was awestruck by the statues and stained glass of Jesus, Mary, and Joseph. I enjoyed hearing the history lessons and the stories of the saints and martyrs. I loved Catholic school. In third grade, we talked about what we wanted to be when we grew up. I raised my hand and said, "I want to be the pope!"

Everyone laughed.

But, hey, if you think about it, I'm still in the running.

So, even though I pursued a love of music and the performing arts early in my college years, there was always a voice, a subtle voice that I've come to know as God's voice in my life, that gently reminded me, I want you to be a priest.

Following that truth, I abruptly quit what seemed to be a bright and promising future as a singer because I always knew my true calling resided in the priesthood. On May 23, 1998, I was ordained for the Ministerial Priesthood of Jesus Christ in the Roman Catholic Church. Serving within the priesthood has been a profound experience, spanning many years. As of today's writing, I am now amid my twenty-fourth year as a priest. One of my assignments was as the pastor in one of the larger parishes within the Diocese of Lexington, Kentucky, which contained a parish, school, and college ministry. When my bishop assigned me as the pastor of St. Mark Catholic Church of Richmond, Kentucky, I arrived to find the church paying off a substantial debt with no reprieve in sight. We discussed ways to relieve the financial burden and tried all the traditional fundraising efforts—ice cream socials, pancake breakfasts, and the famous Catholic Bingo nights. Our efforts didn't even make a dent in the debt.

One morning, I woke up with a crazy and exciting idea. I

would call celebrities and invite them to visit our community to put on performances. We'd sell tickets, and a portion of the proceeds would also be donated to the charity of the celebrities' choice. By God's grace, many of the celebrities I called said yes! We called the events "An Evening Among Friends," and they became a hit. Entertainers visited our small community in Richmond, Kentucky, and seemed to delight in the intimate atmosphere created for our parishioners and fans, who, believe it or not, traveled from all over the world to see the artists perform in such close quarters. Some of the performers who graced our town were TV personality Regis Philbin, comedian Martin Short, musician Natalie Cole, the queen of country, Dolly Parton, former First Lady Barbara Bush, singer and actor Harry Connick Jr., and Vegas showman Donny Osmond, to mention a few. In time, the parish paid off the debt, and charities benefited from donations placed on behalf of the celebrities. Yet, for me, the most profound impact of the events came in the form of newfound friendships, laughter, shared meals, talking, and seeing everyone's walls come down to enjoy themselves and one another.

Interacting with folks and getting to know people I'd otherwise never get the opportunity to meet is also what I enjoy most about traveling, next to my love and passion for sharing the Gospel and preaching the Word of Jesus Christ. Over the years, I've been blessed to travel countless miles around the world, meeting people from all walks of life. For me, one of the best ways to relate to people from all corners of the globe is often through stories. They allow us to step outside of our day-to-day lives for a moment and connect to themes that we can all relate to. We hear a story about a time when someone experienced a moment of embarrassment, such as spending an entire day running errands while wearing a shirt inside out, and then we recall a time when we goofed similarly. (If such moments never happen to you, count your blessings.) I think God recognizes how much I enjoy stories and often places me in the most unusual circumstances to meet genuinely fascinating people. Some of them challenge me in ways that I may not want at the time, but the encounters shift my perspective in ways that God knows I need to better fit into His vastly greater vision.

As I travel to speak from place to place, I can't tell you how many people actually write to my bishop, or the Holy Father, and they say, "How do all those things happen to Father Jim?"

The truth is, they happen to you too! They happen to all of us! The question is, though: Do we have our ears open to hear when God speaks? God moves through all our lives, creating chances for connection, learning, growth, and teaching moments. It is up to us to recognize God's presence. As Jesus proclaimed, "He who has ears, let them hear," and I second that notion, adding that to whomever also has the open eyes, hearts, and minds, may God's presence be revealed. Amen? Amen.

Sharing stories eventually led me to venture into the realm of the written word as an author. I am blessed with many talents; however, sitting down at a desk to hammer out chapter by chapter of a written text seems a far stretch from my God-given skill set. Gratefully though, God provides, and in 2013, along with the help of coauthors, family support, dear friends, and literary professionals, my first book was published, entitled *Among Friends: Stories from the Journey.*

A lot has transpired since then. I completed my twelve-year assignment as pastor of St. Mark Catholic Church in Richmond, Kentucky, and five years ago, my calling changed once again.

Pope Francis called me to serve as one of his Papal Missionaries of Mercy, of which there are one hundred in the United States and roughly nine hundred throughout the world. I am now a full-time traveling evangelist for the Roman Catholic Church.

Although the past few years have brought about many blessings, the time has also presented challenges. My beloved mom, whom I speak of often, died after receiving a diagnosis of aortic stenosis. Her legacy of love, prayer, and service to others lives on in new ways now, and the many lessons she instilled in me continue to inspire many of the stories that I share.

I truly believe that change is inevitable; growth is optional.

Over the past eight years, a lot has changed, and an endless amount of growth within me has taken place. Never did I imagine that a diocesan bishop, let alone a diocesan priest, would be afforded the opportunity of a lifetime: travel the world, preach the Gospel, experience the Catholic Church in a way that possibly mimics, or even exemplifies, precisely what the disciples experienced long ago—traveling from town to town, state to state, country to country, preaching the Good News of Jesus Christ. I live totally out of a suitcase and love it! I jump from one plane to another, ride in a different rental vehicle each week, and try to remember the hotel room of my present location. Some of my colleagues can't believe or even fathom such joy in this, as one of the main charisms of a diocesan priest is to serve rooted in a parish, primarily ministering to those within his local church boundaries. But for those who truly know me, that, at present, is the farthest from where joy resides.

Traveling to preach the Word goes hand in hand with being a Missionary of Mercy and what Pope Francis calls the "New Evangelization," or the "Ministry of Encountering," and suits the personality and gifts with which I've been blessed. For me, it's probably the happiest I've ever been in the twenty-four years of service in the Catholic Church. I say that with gratitude of Bishop Stowe, who, in his knowledge and wisdom, thought outside the box to discern a way for me to best serve the Church. Although I don't have a home parish, I still represent the Diocese of Lexington, Kentucky, wherever my travels take me.

I write this second book at the encouragement of many of you. I do not consider myself anything but a storyteller for God. No prominent theologian, intellectual, or achiever. Actually, those who truly know me know that I struggle with self-worth, identity, and even socializing in public settings. However, the energy I receive from those listening to the Word, attentive to the call, and enriched by the experience of live preaching is where the energy and God's grace are received.

When people ask why I use stories in ministry, I often point back to the example of Jesus. He used stories, that is, parables, that every person of His time could understand. He connected the stories back to a particular teaching. That's what I try to do. At the youngest of ages, we're all told stories. Through stories, we connect back to the beginning of who we are. I'm no different. That's why I have a photo from my first day of kindergarten hanging in the hallway of my home. When I first walk in, I see it, and it reminds me of the dreams I had as a child, and it connects me to who I am in my most authentic expression of self. At that young age, I looked forward not only to playtime but also to story time. I loved sitting around in a circle and listening to Mrs. Richard at St. Mary Catholic School tell stories.

There are those, call them haters or detractors, or what have you, who say, "Look. He's putting the focus on himself." And really, I'm not because it's not about me. It's about God. I share stories of my lived experiences and share photos of these encounters to demonstrate that these are not just coincidences. These are something more. These are examples of God moving through our lives, alive and well.

We can't recognize these moments unless we open ourselves to receive them. We as Catholics receive Jesus each Sunday; through the Word, the sacrament, and one another as everyone partakes in a blessing or receiving the Eucharist. After that, you're sent on your way and asked to be that which you have received—the Body and Blood of Christ. Out into the world. In other words, you're invited to be Christlike. You're invited to be an expression of God. You're asked to go out and live to the best of your ability what you just learned and be your best self.

We're all weak. We're all sinners. We're all broken. Even with all our cracks and our brokenness, we can allow the light of the Holy Spirit to shine through us. We can each be an expression of God in our lives. As we journey together through this book, this collection of stories and encounters with God as I've traveled the globe, sharing the message of Jesus as a Papal Missionary of Mercy for Pope Francis, I intend to prove that God's presence is alive in our world today—and is made available to anyone and everyone. It is up to us as receivers to open our ears, open our eyes, and open our hearts and minds to connect with His presence. It is up to us to come to know the voice of God in our lives, to heed the call when we hear it in our heart of hearts. But here's the thing; He speaks to each of our hearts in ways that only we can understand for ourselves.

I write this book in the hopes of meeting you where you are on any given day. Some stories are meant to uplift or encourage, and others to challenge. The stories jump around in time, and

I share personal reflections along the way. That's intentional—hoping you'll slow down and pause. Whether you read it straight through (as I found many read *Among Friends*) or you read it in small doses, I want you to enjoy the read however you feel called. But I hope you take time with what you read. Talk about it with those in your life and share it with your loved ones. Allow it to awaken your curiosity, draw you nearer to Christ, and open your eyes and your heart to God. Whether you read it in the light of day, or the dark of night, under the bedside lamp, in the sunshine, or in the midst of a storm, I hope you pause to reflect on what you read. Meditate on the feelings you encounter. Because if you sit quietly and listen closely, you just may hear the sound of God's voice. Inviting transformation, calling you to return.

God's presence is accessible to us all, and He may be much closer than you think: for you will never look into the eyes of someone God does not love. Including your own.

Ash Wednesday with the Holy Father

Five years ago, Pope Francis called me to be one of his Missionaries of Mercy; nine hundred fellow priests are similarly appointed throughout the world. People often ask me how Pope Francis called me, and I say, "He picked up the phone and called me. Literally."

The commissioning as a Papal Missionary took place on Ash Wednesday. I received an invitation to Rome, where we celebrated Mass with the Holy Father. I've always found it interesting to consider the weight this individual must carry as the spiritual leader of Roman Catholics, who number roughly 1.34 billion of the 2.5 billion Christians worldwide. As I often say, "I'm only one man." Pope Francis, too, is only one man. Being in his presence, one can immediately notice that he is rooted in prayer. He is one who not only talks the talk but walks the walk of his faith and the message he strives to embody as the Vicar of Christ.

One of the teachings the Holy Father shared with us on Ash

Wednesday was that it's not just about what we give up or sacrifice in life. It's about what we give of ourselves in how we live. We are called to give of ourselves in prayer, in charity, in acts of self-sacrifice, and giving with faith in God's mercy. In other words, all of us have something to offer. This message asks each of us to reflect on our lives and on our actions. Not just on Sundays, but in our everyday lives. It causes us to ask ourselves whether we are sharing our unique, God-given gifts and talents. You see, it costs nothing to be kind. It costs nothing to be compassionate, and it costs nothing to be present with another. It costs nothing to care. We all have something that we can give to another.

The big question that the Holy Father challenged us with was, how can we give more? How can we live more generously and love more deeply? Like in Paul's letter to the Corinthians, he challenged us to be ambassadors of Christ. As a Missionary of Mercy, a Catholic, a human being, how am I to be an ambassador of God for humanity?

The Holy Father gave us a simple guide, but it was also very challenging in its simplicity. He gave us the following three reminders.

Number one: Pause. He reminded us to pause and quiet the noise in our lives. Stop everything in the periphery. Center ourselves away from the distractions and those nagging thoughts—just pause. Take a break.

Number two: See. He reminded us to see with the eyes of Christ. To see people who are struggling and see Christ in the homeless and the despondent. See those who are remorseful and those who are searching for God. He called upon us to see the face of Christ crucified in individuals.

Number three: Return. He reminded us to return without

fear, which, to me, was about the whole concept of giving and receiving, and about revisiting the relationships in our lives. Give without wanting to receive repayment. Return to be with those who you may have forgotten about or with whom you may have disagreed. Return without expectation. Forgive and return to God. Return to church. Return in however you feel called. Just return.

Pause, see, return. As humans, every one of us needs to pause. Every one of us needs to be awakened to see. Every one of us needs to return and to give of ourselves. That is what church is about. We all have something to share as part of a greater community. Right now, the world is in such a *me* mode with social media, and selfie culture, and so on, and yes, for those who know me, I know what you're thinking. I'm guilty of this too. (I share plenty of selfies from my travels throughout this book.) But our church is not a me theology. Our church is a we theology, a communal theology. We are the Catholic Church, which means we are the Universal Church. This means that when someone in the community is in need, I am in need. We are all connected. We are part of the Body of Christ, and the root of our community is Jesus. That's what we believe, and that is why the Eucharist is the foundation of who we are and what we believe as Roman Catholics. That is why everything centers around that Eucharistic table. That's why we not only get fed at the table, but it provides us with enough nourishment to go out into the world as an embodiment of our Lord and Savior, Jesus Christ.

You see, there it comes full circle, back to the message Pope Francis shared. Through the Eucharist, we return to Christ. We return to the community and return out into the world. I think a lot of people can pause and see without too much trouble. The real struggle, I often find, is in returning. I noticed this while traveling to speak through the pandemic. When churches were at partial capacity due to COVID-19, people said, "Why go to church when I can watch it on TV?" Well, I'll tell you something. On TV, we don't get the sense of community, the rootedness, the togetherness that we receive when we actually get up off our butts and go to church. Plus, we don't partake in the Blessed Sacrament, which is at the very core of who we are as Catholics.

We don't always want to make an effort, but we allow God to work through us when we do. Sometimes God brings people into our life or uses us in the lives of others in ways we never imagined. For instance, while I was in Rome, I encountered the Holy Father unexpectedly. At 4:30 a.m., Pope Francis was on his way to the chapel to pray, and I was going to the lobby to catch a cab to the airport. We met at the elevator, where he stopped and looked at me. Then he asked, "Where are you going this early?"

I said, "I'm going out to preach as one of your missionaries to spread the Word of God's mercy, healing, love, and forgiveness."

He then grasped my hands and looked straight into me. You know that gaze when someone really looks into your eyes and truly sees you? That's how he looked at me. He then asked me, well, more accurately, he told me, he said, "Pray for me."

I thought, *Wow, he's asking me for prayer*. He then removed the white zucchetto from his head, placed it in my hands, and said, "Take this wherever you go and remind all of the people you meet, wherever you meet them, that God is with them. God has never and will never abandon them. God's mercy is always theirs."

The words he shared with me five years ago have proven to be prophetic today. I didn't fully understand his words then, or why he specifically said them to me, or why he gave me the gift of his zucchetto. They now resonate with those I encounter who are feeling hopeless or crying out for God's mercy, especially amid a global pandemic, at a time when people are questioning the presence of God. People have experienced significant pain, tragedy, loss, and loneliness. Countless people have suffered and died alone, unable to see loved ones in their final moments. Many feel abandoned by the Church or even the hierarchy because of divisiveness or words of exclusion. However, Pope Francis's message, much like that of Jesus, has brought peace to many during their times of greatest need. Even though I share the message in a Catholic forum 90 percent of the time, the message can be applied in any forum or group 100 percent of the time because we are all human. We are all children of God. We are all called, with no exceptions.

While ministering to those in need, on occasion, I have felt called to place the pope's zucchetto on others as a blessing. It's incredible to witness how the pope's gesture and words have impacted the lives I encounter in the mission for which I was commissioned. (For a testimony of "The Zucchetto," flip to the Testimonies section in the back.) At times, it has brought people to tears, wonder, amazement, humility, even healing. I've placed it on individuals who suffered medical episodes or traumatic brain injuries. Miraculously, they received healing and reconciliation when presented with the zucchetto and Pope Francis's words. Such experiences demonstrate the power of faith. For some, the zucchetto may directly connect people, in a way, to who we as Catholics see as the Vicar of Christ, Pope Francis. The real spark, though, is not necessarily the zucchetto or even the Holy Father's message. Those may serve as a conduit or a catalyst within individuals' lives. Yet it is the activation of one's own belief, one's faith, and the trust in God that moves seemingly impossible mountains in our lives.

As I've traveled in recent years, I feel we're experiencing a remarkable shift in the world and a unique period of growth. Through this time of transition, I find it interesting that the Holy Father chose the name Francis upon the consecration. The Franciscans are known for being visionaries and being prophetic in their work, which often causes people to become unsettled because they dredge up what others wish to remain unstirred. They live simply, and in their simplicity, they call to question the excess and possibly unnecessary practices of others. They put it right there in your face. Inspired by the life and teachings of St. Francis, the Franciscans serve everyone, regardless of background or belief.

Their belief and insistence on the inclusion of everyone, all people, from all walks of life and faith backgrounds, affluence, or the lack thereof are what I find interesting and inspiring. At a time when divisiveness can shift our world into further separation, I believe Pope Francis embodies the message that our world needs today. He embraces all God's children and exemplifies a message of togetherness and a return to the love that Christ professed for us all to share. He challenges those who hold tightly to their righteous views and sense of superiority over their fellow man. He once said, "None of us must feel 'superior' to anyone. None of us should look down at others from above. The only time we can look at a person in this way is when we are helping them to stand up."

The Holy Father pushes people's buttons and does so on purpose to get us to talk, to think, and to get us moving. He truly sees all of humanity as his equal. No one higher and no one lower. At times, that can be disconcerting to many within the hierarchy of the Catholic Church. What he's doing is challenging people to ask themselves, regardless of status, whether they, too, will choose to embody the love of Christ.

I believe that not only does the world want that form of leadership today through this time of transition, but I also believe the world needs it. For me, Pope Francis personifies the message of Christ and leads by powerful example, exemplifying what Christ calls us to do. He seems to love simplicity, and sometimes through simplicity, things can be seen much clearer. He causes us to reevaluate, converse, and stir the passion within us to connect with God. Like Pope Francis's message, and ultimately, the message of Jesus Christ, I believe that every person should be treated with dignity and respect. In the eyes of God, we are all His children. Just because we may be doing well in life doesn't mean God loves us any more or less than the person living on the streets. Pope Francis, by his example, reminds us, "Whatever you do to the least of my brother and sisters, you do to me."

As a Papal Missionary of Mercy, Pope Francis has charged me with a Ministry of Encountering. This book is an expansion of that charge appointed to me. As Catholics, as individual embodiments of the Body of Christ, and as human beings; mothers, brothers, sisters, fathers, wives and husbands, sons and daughters, relatives, friends, coworkers, and the many roles we each live within our journey alongside God, I, in turn, challenge you to a life of encountering. A life of recognizing God's presence as He appears in your life—equally in the miraculous events and the everyday situations.

Through the pages of this book, we will share stories, which I hope will bring smiles, bring laughter, and maybe even a few tears of reconciliation. But, most of all, I hope the stories serve as your own personal encounters with God.

Encountering God

#60MinutesforJesus

I present most of my traveling ministry over three days in an event I call "#60MinutesforJesus." Those who previously attended my talks know that I stick to sixty minutes only, and precisely that. Why? Because I find that amount of time very tolerable for people. Sixty minutes sounds much more accessible to partake in than an hour. Not sure why, but it does. If you think about it, God, our Creator, gives us twenty-four hours a day, seven days a week, three hundred and sixty-five days a year. Why can't you just give back sixty minutes for Jesus? You know, the Man who hung on a cross, died from blunt force trauma, asphyxiation, and a lack of blood in His love for you? Sixty minutes. A very minor ask in the grand scope of time. I promise people no more and no less at the events, and I remain steadfast to that promise. I expect people to take off their hats, sit up straight in the pews, take the toys and the snacks away from the children, and really bring their full presence. It's only sixty minutes, after all.

The first night of the live events speaks about the root of the Gospel: love and kindness, and how Jesus exemplified that in His life and teachings. When asked which is the greatest commandment in the law, Jesus replied, in Mathew 22:37, "Love the Lord your God with all your heart and with all your soul and with all your mind." And the second-greatest commandment He gave us, "You shall love your neighbor as yourself." To really exemplify that, you have to learn to be kind. During the three nights together, and now, throughout this text, we discuss three ways in which kindness can be expressed.

Number one: Don't be a jerk. In other words, realize that lives are messy. There's always something happening in the privacy of our lives that others know nothing about! Maybe we're not feeling well. Our boss did something we don't like. Our children are unhappy. I'm mad at my spouse. The list of possibilities for how our lives can be messy can go on and on. That doesn't mean we have to pass on our messiness to others. I remember a hectic time on the road when my flight was delayed due to bad weather. I felt exhausted from the previous connecting flight and was just completely over the whole situation. I remember talking to my bishop, and I said, "Bishop, my life is a cross."

To which he responded, "Really, Jim? For you or for others?" (I don't even know what that means to this day.)

I interpreted his response as a reminder: you don't have to pass on your misery to others.

Some of the most incredible God experiences happen to me when I'm being a jerk. God will place someone in my life, or me in theirs, to redirect our hearts. I call those moments "Encounters with God," or "God Moments." Those moments when God's presence becomes so real, so vivid, that I know without a doubt

He is with me, among us—redirecting my heart and teaching me to be better, more authentic, and true.

Number two: Honor the absent. What that means, plain and simple: stop the gossip. Nothing degrades one's own spiritual life more than gossip. Nothing is more humiliating than pulling down the life of someone else, especially when they are not present and unable to speak for themselves. To do so is a severe form of being uncharitable. Every one of us is going through something no one else knows about. If you have something to say about someone, say it to their face; and that doesn't mean you have to do it rudely.

It's not confrontation. It's conversation.

Keep in mind, and this is often the hard part of a conversation for some of us, when you speak to someone about an issue you may have with them, after you share the matter, shut your mouth and listen. Open your ears and listen to what the person says. The root of the issue may, in fact, have nothing to do with what you thought. It may have nothing to do with them and everything to do with you!

Number three: Always give people the benefit of the doubt, a teaching taken from the spiritual exercises of St. Ignatius of Loyola. In other words, when someone asks you something, think positively instead of negatively, unless you factually know otherwise.

Don't be a jerk. Honor the absent. Always give people the benefit of the doubt.

Simple, right? . . . Wrong!

When people ask me about the three teachings from #60MinutesforJesus events, I say, "They're extremely simple. They're so simple, they're difficult." In truth, similar to the three teachings that Pope Francis shared on Ash Wednesday, everyone can apply the three teachings that I share and relate to them in their own way. That's why when I speak, children, parents, and the elderly fill the audience. All are welcome and invited. The three simple teachings can relate to everyone. That's the beauty of #60MinutesforJesus: no one is excluded. I tell people, "If there are elderly among you, you should be the ones to call them and bring them. If there are people here who are sick, you should go out and get them." I don't like the three nights being livestreamed or taped because people then use that as an excuse not to attend, and the whole point of #60MinutesforJesus is to break people out of their routine and into church for three consecutive nights. Worshipping, singing, laughing, crying, and all being together in the house of the Lord.

It's not just Catholics who show up. People come up to me and say, "I'm from a Baptist church." Or they will say, "I'm not from any church."

All are welcome. I often ask people who attend the events, "If you see someone here you don't know, are you welcoming them to your community?"

After attending the three days of talks, I hope people feel inspired, challenged, lightened (enlightened, but also lightened of burdens they may carry that day), and entertained in a very unique way that allows for learning.

I write books and share stories through the written word for similar reasons.

It's humbling when I meet people and they say they've read my book or have given a copy to their children. Really though, for me, writing and sharing stories is a way to bring God's Word to people who may not experience the teachings live, in person.

And for those who do attend in person, it's a way to take home the teachings, sit with them, meditate on them, and hopefully offer further reflections on their relationship with God. It's a form of what Pope Francis calls the Ministry of Encountering. Or the Ministry of Presence. The ministry I am called to serve is about being with people, being with the faithful, and interacting with people from all walks of life. Not just those who believe like us or think like us. To not only share God's Word but to listen.

When asked "Where is God?," many people will say, "God is up in the sky," or "Somewhere up there." If someone asked you "Where is God?," what would you say? My response is, "Look. Look around you. God is all around us. He's in the homeless just as He's in the rich. He's not just in the poor, the meek, and the imprisoned. He is everywhere, and He makes himself known to us every day. He's in the beauty of the trees. He's in the storm. He's in the destruction and in the rebirth. He's even in what we consider death. He's in the triumphs, yes, but we must also remember that He's there with us in the defeats. He's in the eyes of everyone we meet."

God is all around us and dwells within each of us. That is the real presence of God. I often find that God appears to us in the people and places we least expect and when we are most in need. And as we recently experienced through the COVID-19 global pandemic (which hopefully, by the time you read this, will be a distant memory in the past), God's message through Christ and God's Word is always there for everyone. In times of celebration and sorrow, and every moment in between, one constant we can always count on is God's love for us all.

Preaching Through the Pandemic

Travel never stopped for me during the pandemic. As a traveling Missionary of Mercy, I witnessed firsthand the state of our nation. People continued to attend Mass, albeit in smaller numbers due to capacity limitations, and attendees wore masks. I will never forget the experiences I had during the height of COVID-19, as I imagine most of us won't either.

During my travels, the pandemic seemed to highlight the importance of community in our world. We stopped seeing people publicly at church, at the office, or at sporting events. Even children stayed home from school. We just stopped. Our society slowed down, and I think that proved difficult for many people. By pausing our busy, prepandemic schedules, COVID brought into awareness aspects of our lives that needed healing. It made us realize areas of our lives that we took for granted.

The inability to gather and be a part of the greater community seemed to ignite a desire to return to togetherness. The lack of connectedness, being among friends, family, and loved ones, proved to be one of the most challenging aspects of the pandemic for many people. Recognizing that lack, people began to find a new appreciation for the simple aspects of life. Families started eating together again around the dinner table. I think people realized, *Wow, were we really that busy before? What did we fill our time with before COVID? Why did we not take time for one another? Or if we did, why did we take it for granted?*

We took for granted so many aspects of our lives. We took for granted those who serve us in our communities. We took for granted the ability to go to church. Did you ever imagine, before COVID, the inability to attend church? Did you ever imagine not being able to be with loved ones in their dying moments? Did you ever think that our health-care workers would be pushed to such extremes to care for us? The extreme circumstances we all faced caused us to slow down and to take a deeper look. I believe the awareness brought about by the unexpected global events created a newfound sense of appreciation in many people.

When jobs vanished and work opportunities halted, people rediscovered an appreciation for their previous position or discovered a desire to pursue another job or another career entirely! People appreciated working in an office, or others appreciated the opportunity to work from home. The changes made us look more closely at what mattered to us. The shift in our daily lives reminded us of the importance of helping one another and the role of community. The collective experience of loss, disconnection, and change invited us to return to gratitude. As challenging as the circumstances were to us all, each in our own ways, our experiences reminded us to appreciate the people and the blessings present in our lives. In tragedy, we are reminded to be thankful for all that God provides. We are reminded to turn to God with gratitude.

Thankfully, the ministry provided to me never stopped during COVID-19. I traveled and continued #60MinutesforJesus amid the pandemic. In ministry, I noticed people's hunger for hope. Their desire for truth, especially when so much seemed uncertain. People longed to be encouraged again. They wanted to laugh and to get back to the lives we lived before the pandemic. Will life ever be the same? We don't know. We only know to trust God and His vision for our lives. Through stable times and times of change and periods of turbulence, we can always count on God.

Remember: Friends come and go. God comes and stays.

Like anyone, I have experienced times when I questioned God's plan and what the future holds. However, never ever during the pandemic did I experience doubt or succumb to fear for lack of faith in God's will for us. I continued doing the best I knew how. I did what I could to adapt to the changing circumstances and continued traveling, sharing Christ's message in a creative fashion.

In one event, I spoke to attendees in a parking lot. People parked cars in front of a stage, and I preached. Seriously! I spoke into a microphone, and people tuned in to their radios to hear my talk. (You can see a photo of me preaching to the parking lot in the Image Gallery.) I also spent time in a COVID-19 hospital unit, wearing multiple layers of masks and protective gear, ministering to health-care workers and those sick with the virus. (There's a picture with the first responders in the Image Gallery.) Did the circumstances require me to adjust? Absolutely. Did the message I share, or the Word of God change? Not at all.

The Word of God cannot be suppressed.

In other words, we changed. Yet the Word of God remained the same. The format changed. I never imagined preaching outdoors to a parking lot filled with cars, but even during the pandemic, what I preached and the message I preached didn't change. Society has changed tremendously since the time of Jesus. Lifestyles and life spans changed in magnitudes, and technology continues to expand into new horizons, and yet, still, the Gospel remains as relevant today as it was in the lives of the disciples. The Gospel speaks to us and delivers us truth, encouragement, and guidance, no matter the circumstances we go through. As we move beyond the pandemic and into whatever the future may hold for us all, I know one thing, my brothers and sisters, the Word of God prevails. The Word of God remains eternal.

We are not supposed to change any part of the Gospel. However, the Gospel is supposed to change every part of us.

Another of the remarkable experiences I had during the pandemic was noticing how blessed we are to have such incredible people serving as first responders, operating on the front lines during times of crisis. These first responders suited up, day and night, tirelessly battling COVID-19 to heal the sick, risking their own lives in the process. To our men and women in uniform, police officers, firefighters, doctors, nurses, and to all first responders who serve our communities keeping us safe each day and night, I am deeply grateful for your service. Thank you. The following prayer is for first responders:

> *Almighty God we pray to you,*
> *In heaven up above.*
> *Watch over our dear first responders,*

And protect them with your love.
Please guide them as they keep us,
Safe both day and night.
And hold them firmly in your care,
Should danger come their way.
Give them true strength and courage,
As they serve till duty's end.
And one more thing to ask dear Lord,
Protect their family and friends.

Who Saw Christ Through You Today?

I don't know if you have them where you live, the people holding signs, asking for food. Or asking for money. People come up to me all the time and ask me, "Father, should I give them money?"

I always ask them in return, "What does your heart tell you to do?"

They say, "To give them money."

"Then give them money," I say.

Then they often respond, "But, Father, I don't want to help their alcoholism!"

I ask, "What, are you in AA with them?"

You see, God judges us by *our* hearts—not by their heart or by their actions.

I'll share with you a fantastic story. I don't know if you've ever heard of the National Prayer Breakfast in Washington, D.C. When I attended in 2015, everyone who is anyone was there.

Everyone I see on TV was there. The president, the first lady, and over three thousand people were gathered at the Washington Hilton. Oh my gosh, I took selfies with everyone! I met people I agree with and people I disagree with politically. You can still respect people, no matter what they believe.

I ran around with my phone in hand, flagging down people I recognized, saying, "Oh my gosh, Nancy Pelosi! We need to talk, but let's take a selfie!" Then I'd see Paul Ryan and run after him and say, "Wow, look at that, you do work out. Let's take a picture!" Then I saw the Dalai Lama. I bowed quickly and said, "Can I take your picture?" (The picture's in the Image Gallery.)

I preached there to the gathered crowd, and after we finished, the Secret Service took me all around Washington, D.C., on a private tour in my clerics. And let me tell you something, I looked sharp that day. I really did. I went to Supercuts beforehand and got my hair cut. I went to Walmart and bought these fake cuff links. The kind that snap on, you know?

They took me back to the hotel around 4:30 p.m. I stepped out of the car, said my goodbyes to the Secret Service, and as I walked toward the entrance of the hotel, out of the corner of my eye, I saw a young man. He looked to be about twenty-three years old and homeless. Who was he walking toward? Can you guess? Me! The priest, walking in my clerics. What did I do? I kept walking. He called out, "Father!"

Finally, I turned to him and said, "Yes?"

He came up to me and said, "Do you have any money?"

I told him, "No. I don't carry cash on me." Which is true. I don't. I never have and never do. I only have two credit cards; one is a gas card for Shell, and the other is a Visa. That's it.

So when this young man asked me if I had any money, I didn't. I said to him, "Are you hungry?"

He said, "I'm starved."

I said, "Would you like to have dinner with me?"

He said, "I'd love to."

I turned and held out my arm and said, "Well, look. Across the street, there's an Italian restaurant. Let's go there. Will you eat with me?"

He said, "Sure."

I quickly got on my phone, trying to Yelp it. It was a five-star Italian restaurant. I'm Italian. I don't know what background you may come from, but as an Italian, I knew what I was getting into by putting my foot in my mouth, suggesting a five-star Italian restaurant.

The maître d' greeted me at the entrance in a rush, rapidly speaking Italian, "Hey, Padre. *Come va?* Hey! *Bene, grazie!*" You know? It was the whole boisterous Italian greeting with the hand gestures. He brought me into the restaurant, and you know what he did? He shut the door on the homeless guy.

I said, "*Mi scusi. Mi scusi.* No, no, no, he's with me."

If you don't know Italians, let me tell you something. When they get angry, you know it because their hands start going everywhere. You know what he did? He made us wait outside. Five minutes later, he came to escort us to our table, and guess where he sat us? If you're thinking to yourself that he sat us in the kitchen—no. I wish he sat us in the kitchen! That would be a place of honor for an Italian. He sat us in the storage closet. I'm not joking. We were seated at a makeshift table next to the toilet plunger. Next to the toilet paper. Next to the disinfectants. It was a cardboard table with a white tablecloth draped over it and two folding chairs. When I saw where he sat us, my heart sank. I was never more embarrassed and humiliated in my entire life.

I tried to make light of the situation. I turned to the homeless young man and said, "Excuse me. What do you do? Do you have any idea how expensive it is to get a private dining room in a restaurant like this?"

Our food was served, and the boy ate. He ate, and he ate like I've never seen anyone eat before. Then we left. As we walked out, I realized that I never asked him his name through the course of our whole conversation.

I said, "Excuse me. What is your name?"

He said, "My name is Kyle, Father."

I said, "Kyle, do you want to take a selfie?"

Let me tell you something. Kyle lit up! He lit up like I've never seen anyone light up before. I asked him, "Kyle, why are you lighting up like that?"

He said to me, "Father, if you want to take a selfie with me, then it means that I matter to someone."

This was a twenty-three-year-old kid.

I said to him, "Kyle, you do matter to someone. Most importantly, you matter to God. Just because you're going through a rough time today doesn't mean that God has abandoned you. You and I have the same DNA as God. Do you understand me? You and I are brothers, Kyle. And don't you ever forget that!" (See Kyle in the Image Gallery.)

Since that day, I've never seen Kyle again. What I can tell you, without a shred of doubt, is that his face, as you can see in the selfie we took together, is the face of Jesus Christ.

"Whatever you do to the least of my brothers and sisters, you do to me."

Sometimes that voice speaks in much less subtle ways. Like, for example, before I answered the call to join the priesthood, back in my college days in Boston, I got called into Symphony Hall for rehearsal. I waited for the subway car, shivering, along with a sea of people during rush hour. As the train came to a stop, I squeezed into the subway car, wedging myself between two people. (You have to be aggressive in big cities; no one moves to make space for you.)

An odor filled the air as the doors shut: an odor that smelled like an unwashed body, onions, and a bathroom urinal rolled into one putrid scent. People wrapped scarves around their noses. I even heard a few people gag.

I looked through the crowd of people to see a disheveled homeless man. His gray beard, matted and full of dirt, came down to his chest. The poor man's watery red eyes suggested an addiction of some kind, most likely alcohol.

To my shame, I prayed, *Dear God, please don't send that man my way. Because, God, we've discussed this. You constantly send these people to me, and I'm not ready for it. In Jesus's name, Amen.*

Sometimes, God hears our prayer and answers us directly with, *No.*

God said, *Not today, Jim.*

As soon as I said, *Amen*, the man looked at me and started walking. This man parted the crowd like the Red Sea in that subway car, and he looked straight at me. An unusual intensity in his eyes.

As the car came to the next stop at Copley Square, he reached out to me and asked me a question. Intentionally, I turned my back on him, ignoring him. He was covered in fecal matter, stained with urine, and full of open sores. I couldn't even bear to face him.

As the car came to an abrupt stop, he slammed into a woman wearing a white mink coat, and he simply asked her, "Do you have a quarter?"

The woman gave him a dollar.

The doors opened on the subway. The man stepped down, and immediately—within a millisecond—a voice came into my head: *James William Sichko—if that were my Son, you also denied him.*

Tears came flowing out of my eyes. I jumped off the subway without a heartbeat's hesitation. I followed after him into the crowd, milliseconds after he stepped out of the car. The man disappeared. I don't mean disappeared into the crowd. I mean, he vanished into thin air.

No one can convince me this man wasn't an angel or maybe even Christ himself.

Don't believe me? Read Psalm 2. The Kingdom of God is for the weak, and Jesus is the face of those people.

How well do you recognize that in your own life? Do you detest the lowest of the low? Do you believe yourself somehow superior? How would Jesus have responded to that man on the subway? How would you have responded to him?

Proverbs 19:17 tells us, "Whoever is kind to the poor lends to the Lord, and He will reward them for what they have done." And Proverbs 21:13 reminds us, "Whoever shuts their ears to the cry of the poor will also cry out and not be answered."

In God's eyes, we are all His children, and everything we have is given to us by God. At a moment's notice, it can all be gone. We never know the struggles that others have faced. Who are we to judge them in their suffering?

Judge nothing, you will be happy.

Forgive everything, you will be happier.

Love everything, you will be happiest.

Who are we to know what has led them astray or to lose sight of the Lord? Or, if we're honest with ourselves, could it even be us who has lost sight of the Lord? And it's not only about the homeless, or the poor, or the imprisoned. It's not always about the extreme circumstances. Sure, sometimes, the drastic encounters can speak to our hearts at a moment's notice. Other times, though, recognizing that we can see one another through the loving eyes of Jesus can happen with those much closer to us.

Who are those people in your life you've turned your back on? Someone must come to mind. What difference of opinion caused you to deny them? What disagreement caused you to ignore the humanity and God's presence within them. For people on the right side of politics, it might be that progressive who voted for Biden or Bernie Sanders. Or, on the other side of politics, it might be the conservative who voted for Trump. What about the gay or transgender person everyone picks on at school? Or how about the bully who stops at nothing to embarrass or harass others?

Even them. All of them. Can we find a way to "love thy neighbor" despite our differences? Just as Jesus loves each one of us. Beyond the urge to turn our backs and to deny in fear, or self-preservation, or our sense of righteousness. Fear, my brothers and sisters, is not of God. With God, and through God, all things are possible. And underneath it all, we are all human, children of God in His eyes.

The truth is, we may disagree. We may not see eye to eye. We may not have the same beliefs or the same priorities. We may not view things the same but that doesn't mean I don't care what you think. That doesn't mean we can't get along. That doesn't mean you are any less deserving of my kindness. In a world where opinions seem to be dividing us more and more, let's remember our humanity. Let's treat others the same way we want to be treated. We don't have to agree—but we should always be kind.

We seem as a society, a nation, even as a world, and, yes, sadly, as a church at times, to "lock the door" or "close the door" on anyone who is not like us. All too often, people turn their backs on those who do not look like us, act like us, or fit our definition of what it means to be a Catholic, a Christian, or even a person. Thinking in such a way is the furthest thing from living like the example set for us by the life of Jesus Christ. Yet we see this happen all the time. Christian prosperity preachers such as Joel Osteen preach that all people are created equal, and everyone goes to heaven because God loves everyone the same. However, when Houston was underwater recently, people were displaced by the flood and looking for refuge. They came knocking on the doors to Osteen's megachurch complex because it was high and dry, above the waters. Did he open the doors to those in need? No. He locked the doors and turned people away.

What do you think Jesus would have done? Or better yet, if you were in the same situation, would you have opened your doors? Similarly, immigration has become a global crisis, and a hot-button issue for many Americans. I don't know how you feel about it, but I think you might know how Jesus would respond to the issue . . . with love and compassion. Personally, I'd much rather live next door to someone who crossed a desert to become an American than an American who wouldn't cross the street to help a foreigner.

As one who travels throughout the world every day, I can tell you something. Our world has turned increasingly nasty. We have become an angry people. It is my goal through Pope Francis and the help of the Holy Spirit to spread mercy, and joy, and kindness, even in my own sinfulness, through the grace of the Eucharist and the sacraments. It costs nothing to be kind, for any one of us, my brothers and sisters. It's something that we can all do, if only we're willing. Let me ask you a question, and please, be honest with yourself. Who today saw Jesus Christ through you?

Who today was led to Jesus, not by your speech, but by your actions? By your joy? By your love? By your capacity for compassion? Who was moved to see Jesus through you today and thought, *I want* that?

Don't Be a Boat Potato

Much of what plagues our world today comes when we fear, and if you think about it, the same was true during the time of the Bible. In Genesis, Adam and Eve lived in perfect harmony with God in the Garden of Eden, utterly free of fear—until when? That's right. When they ate the forbidden fruit from the tree of knowledge, and they became afraid. Sin was introduced to the world, and instantly, fear disrupted their harmony with God.

In modern times, fear comes in all shapes and sizes. Sometimes we fear rejection and criticism from others, or we fear change or fear one another for any multitude of reasons. We may even fear ideological or cultural differences held by others. I've noticed that our culture has accepted two huge lies. One, if you disagree with someone's lifestyle, you must fear or hate them. Two, if you love someone, it means you agree with everything they believe and do. In my opinion, both concepts are nonsense. You do not have to compromise your personal convictions to be compassionate. Pope Francis clearly stated his thoughts about fear when he said, "We must not allow fear to rule our lives."

Moses was afraid when God told him to leave his humble profession as a shepherd to confront Pharaoh and demand the release of the Israelites. Yet Moses didn't allow fear to rule his life. Instead, he acted with courage and faith, and because he chose to act in the face of fear, he forever altered the course of history.

Fear keeps us in the boat, stuck and unable to move forward in our lives. The Bible gives us the unlikely example of Peter to help us not let fear rule our lives. Saint Peter wouldn't have been my first pick. He was not the most prayerful or the smartest. He probably smelled of fish and was quick to speak when he should have left well enough alone. Nope, I wouldn't have picked him. Good thing Jesus didn't ask my opinion. But one thing about Peter is he was willing to risk and was prepared to take a chance. Jesus knew this about Peter. Jesus knew there was more to Peter than just what was on the surface. He knew every bit of Peter's sinfulness and brokenness. He knew Peter would put his foot in his mouth. He knew Peter would deny Him—yet He still chose him. He chose him because He knew what was possible with Peter, and eventually, Peter the sinner became Peter the saint.

You and I are like Peter. We can probably think of a million reasons why God shouldn't call us or choose us. The thing is, you and I *have* been called and chosen. Despite our brokenness. Despite our sinfulness. Despite not knowing everything about everything. We are enough. We have been chosen by God to be His instrument, His hands, His feet, His messengers of mercy. He knows our hearts better than we do, and He knows what is possible if we "cast our nets" and trust Him. We can lean on the excuses that keep us from reaching our full potential, or we can be like Peter, and with God's grace and mercy and love, become great saints. I really wouldn't have picked Peter, but what do I know . . .

Do you recall the story of Peter walking on water?

The disciples went fishing one day. They were in small boats on the Sea of Galilee when a massive storm loomed overhead. Jesus, who didn't join them on the trip, appeared to them and walked on the water toward them. The disciples were a bit surprised, to say the least, and no one said anything.

That was, except Peter.

We need to remember something significant about this story. Peter suggested that he, himself, walk on water. Peter called out, "Jesus, if it's really You, tell me to come to you across the water."

Jesus told him, "Come on out, Peter."

What do you think all the apostles in the boat did at that moment? You know they probably laughed at his expense and criticized him. "Yeah, Peter, go on out there. You're the one who opened your mouth—just like you're always doing, Peter."

But Peter did it; he got out of the boat. Because at that moment, Peter possessed a deep trust in Jesus. Peter had spent a lot of time with Jesus, so he understood what Jesus was capable of. Peter watched as Jesus raised people from the dead. He saw Jesus heal the sick and perform miracles before his eyes. He knew what Jesus could do, so when Jesus appeared to the apostles, walking on water, Peter trusted him. And Jesus, in turn, knew what Peter was capable of . . . and what he wasn't.

So, what happened? Do you remember?

He submitted to Jesus. He surrendered and stepped from the boat to walk on water.

But then what happened after he took his first step? Yep, you're right—he sank.

He did. But here's the thing. He tried because he believed. He had faith, and he acted. Peter knew that walking on water was humanly impossible. But he submitted to follow Christ's lead, His teaching, His calling, and Jesus's invitation.

Then, fear got the better of him.

One aspect of this story that people often overlook is the eleven other individuals who knew Jesus, who experienced Jesus and what He could do, and saw Jesus at that moment on the water but chose to stay in the boat. They didn't get out. They didn't risk.

I wonder, how many of us reading this story are like those eleven apostles, or what I like to call "boat potatoes"? And a further question: What hinders us from getting out of the boat? What prevents us from really embracing God? I don't mean embracing God when it suits us—no! I'm talking about embracing God in the fullness of who we are. That's the point of the Eucharist, of Holy *Communion*. In Communion, we are invited to join with the Body and the Blood of Jesus Christ, to *commune* and embrace God in wholeness. The word *holy* derives from the old English root *hāl*, which referred to health and wholeness. To love God and embrace God in the wholeness of our being is akin to holiness.

From Pope Francis in *Gaudete et Exsultate*, the five signs of holiness in today's world are: one, perseverance, patience, and meekness; two, joy and humor; three, boldness and passion; four, community; and five, constant prayer.

Often, sadly, it's the doubt and the fear of criticism from the people closest to us that we allow to grow and permeate within us. In the words of politician and activist John Lewis, "Never let anyone—any person or any force—dampen, dim or diminish your light." It is up to us to become aware of the fear we allow into our lives. To do so, we must take a look at why we do some of the things we do. (Or allow others to do.)

How many times do we repeat the same patterns, over and over in our lives, without really knowing why we do it? We usually sit in the same seat at church. We go to the same restaurants. We don't want to risk because we may have a bad experience. It wasn't all that great for Peter, either. He sank, but also, he was saved.

It's like the story of my sister's pot roast. Every time she cooks pot roast, she always cuts off the ends of the meat, then wraps it in aluminum foil and puts it in the oven. After watching her do this several times, I finally asked, "Why do you do that?"

She said, "Because that's how Mom always made it." Then she shrugged and said, "That's how I was taught."

I asked her, "Well, why did Mom do that?"

She said, "I don't know."

I called Mom and asked her, "Mom, why did you always cut both ends off the pot roast?"

She said simply, "I cut off both ends because the roast we bought would never be able to fit in our oven."

Turns out, the ovens were much smaller when my mom taught my sister how to cook the roast. For years, my sister wasted parts of the roast just because that was how she had always done it, without knowing why.

How many areas of our lives are similar? How much of our life is being underutilized simply because *that's how we've always done it*?

We tend to remain in our comfort zones because *that's how*

we've always done it, and let's face it, it's easier that way. It's comfortable. It makes things less complicated. But that doesn't mean it's always right. That doesn't mean it's always efficient, and when it comes to our eating habits, that certainly doesn't mean it's always nutritious. In fact, getting out of our comfort zones provides discomfort and challenge. But there's nothing wrong with that. Challenge doesn't have to be a "negative" thing. Why isn't challenge seen as a good thing? I think we avoid challenges at times because it requires us to change. Change moves us from where we are to where we could be, and that can be scary.

What does God say about fear? That's right, "Be not afraid."

Growth doesn't happen in our comfort zones. We must examine these aspects of ourselves if we want to grow and allow God to fully utilize us for our fullest potential. There is no way you will grow and expand the horizons for your life if you don't take that step that Peter did—if you don't risk.

All God asks of us is that we trust as Peter trusted. God asks us to step out of our man-made boats, our comfort zones, and the criticisms of ourselves or the criticisms of others. God asks us to step out of our doubts and our fears and simply, to try. When we do, He takes our halting, stumbling efforts and transforms them into something beautiful. You see, God doesn't ask for perfection. He just asks us to step out of our little boats and join Him.

Russell

When you genuinely love God and trust God, He will call you out of your comfort zone. The only way you will get out of your comfort zone is if you risk. There's no other way. And to risk, you're going to have to trust, and that requires communication. That's why I constantly ask the question, "Do you know the voice of God in your life?"

If I asked you, "What has been, and what is, the sound of God's voice in your life?," would you know and be able to tell me?

Let me share something with you. I do know the way God speaks to me. But the way God speaks to me will be different from the way God speaks to you. God speaks the language of our own, unique hearts.

Let me tell you a story of a time when I heard that familiar call, that tug at my heart, and I trusted God. I was speaking in Glen Ellyn, Illinois. At the end of the mission, they took up an offering. If anyone writes a check to me, I handwrite thank-you

notes and put them in the mail, same day. That's just what I do.
It's what my parents taught me. You don't write an email. You
handwrite a note. That's what I do when I'm on a plane—always
wearing my hoodie and my sandals and shorts. After speaking
in Glen Ellyn, I was flying from Illinois to Pittsburgh, Pennsylvania, to speak at the William Penn Hotel for an event hosted
by the Pittsburgh Steelers organization. (Sorry if you're not a
Steelers fan.)

While on the plane, I looked at one of the checks taken up at
the offering in Glen Ellyn and noticed a check for $1,000. That
is huge for my mission. The memo line had a number sign, followed by the word *cell*, and then a phone number. So, naturally,
I texted them, "Dear Mr. and Mrs. Matthew Baker, this is Father
Jim. Thank you for the $1,000 donation. I'm off to Pittsburg
today. Please know of my prayers." Then I sent the message.

Three minutes later, *ding*! I received a response. "Father Jim,
we're in Pittsburgh, Pennsylvania. We left after the second night
of your talk because our twenty-three-year-old nephew is dying
of liver cancer. He is unchurched. He is at Allegheny General
Hospital. Will you pray for him?"

I texted back, "Be assured of my prayers."

When I landed in Pittsburgh, what did my heart tell me to
do? It told me to go visit their nephew. But what did my mind
tell me to do? Not go. I couldn't. I didn't have time. I had a speaking engagement for three thousand people at the William Penn
Hotel, and I was the keynote speaker.

What do you do in such a situation?

You follow your heart. If your heart is sound and informed,
you always follow your heart. Because you trust. That's where
miracles can happen in our lives. So I jumped in the Hertz rental

car and drove seventy miles in the opposite direction. Four miles from the Allegheny General Hospital, a Pennsylvania state trooper pulled me over. It wasn't my first rodeo, being pulled over for speeding. (Sadly!) I took out the rental car agreement and my driver's license and looked in the rearview mirror. What did I see? A young, brand-new trooper. That's awful. You know why? They follow *everything* by the books.

Here came the young trooper, walking up to my driver-side door. I handed him my driver's license and registration. He leaned toward my window and very mildly asked, "Excuse me? Do you know why I pulled you over?"

I said, "Nope. Sorry, no idea. . . ." I wasn't going to give him ammunition!

He said, "Is there an emergency?"

I said, "Yes, there is. There's a young man, twenty-three years old, unchurched, who is dying of liver cancer at Allegheny General Hospital."

He asked, "Is it one of your parishioners?"

I thought, *Hello? I'm not from here! Read the license!* I didn't say that, of course. Instead, I said, "No, he's not."

He said, "Well, then how do you know him?"

"I don't know him," I responded. "His aunt and uncle gave me a thousand-dollar check."

He said, "Oh, so you know the aunt and uncle?"

"No! I don't know the aunt and uncle either! Please, just write the ticket and send me on my way. I'm in a hurry." I showed him the text from Mr. and Mrs. Matthew Baker. I said, "His name is Russell."

The trooper said to me, "Father, Russell is my younger brother."

He escorted me to the hospital, where I baptized Russell. I gave Russell his first Holy Communion. Confirmed Russell. Anointed Russell. Three weeks later, along with the bishop in Pittsburgh, Pennsylvania, at St. Paul Cathedral in downtown Pittsburgh, I buried Russell.

Do you see? You never know.

To truly see, we must T.R.U.S.T. We must spend *time* with God to form a *relationship*. That brings *understanding*, which allows us to *surrender* to His will, and then all we have to do is *try*. It would have been easy for me to listen to my head instead of my heart when I landed in Pittsburgh, but I would have been ignoring what I knew to be the voice of God in my life. How often is God speaking to you in your own life? And how often have you responded with your head and not your heart? Only you, and God, can know the truth within your heart.

Blessings Come to
Those Who Risk

I spoke outside of New Orleans in a town alongside the Mississippi River called Chalmette, Louisiana. Being by the riverside, down in the delta, the town has been affected by numerous storms. The people of Chalmette have been through a lot in recent years. I was invited to preach at their parish, and it was the first time they had gathered as a congregation during COVID.

While there, I presided at a Mass for the schoolchildren. Those who have seen me speak at #60MinutesforJesus know that I often call on people sitting in the pews and ask them questions. During Mass, I called on a young boy in the sixth grade to ask him a question. Interestingly, before I called on this young boy, the teacher signaled for the boy to put his hand down, but the boy kept raising his hand. So, of course, I called on him. I said out loud to the teacher, "Ma'am, please don't interfere in this."

I asked the youngster the question, and surprisingly, he got it right. As I usually do when someone answers a question correctly when put on the spot in my talks, I gave him a gift card. I decided to pursue it a little further. I invited him to the ambo and began to ask him some other questions. He wasn't sure about the answers to the new questions, but something told me to work with this young kid. There's this game that I play called Double or Nothing. This is how the game works: the "contestants" can either go for a question and receive an additional gift card to the one they've already won, or they can choose to walk away with the one gift card.

I asked the boy, "Do you want to go for double or nothing?"

He said, "No, Father. I'm staying with what I got."

I said, "Are you *really* sure? Because I believe there's something in you that tells me you know this."

He again politely declined and said, "No, thank you, Father."

I persisted and said, "I'm going to give you one more chance."

He finally relented and said, "Okay, I'll go for it."

I asked him a follow-up question about the sacraments of the church. Lo and behold, he got the answer wrong. So I snatched back the original gift card from his hand.

He wasn't upset. He laughed, and even though I had just taken back his gift card, he still said, "Thank you, Father."

There was something about this young boy that made me offer another chance for him to win. I said, "We can do something if you're up to it. We can phone a friend of mine, and they can possibly help you. If you and my friend get the answer right, you'll win both gift cards. If you wish to."

He scrolled through the contacts in my phone and selected a retired priest named Father Frank. He called Father Frank on speakerphone, in front of all the students, and asked him the question. Father Frank gave him some insights into the question.

I asked the boy, "Do you want to go with Father Frank's answer?"

He said, "Yes."

The answer was correct, and he won both gift cards.

Usually, the Double or Nothing game ends there, but there was just something compelling about this young man. Something told me to ask him, "Have you selected where you're going to high school?"

In that diocese, students started high school in the eighth grade. He told me that he had been accepted to De La Salle High School.

I said to him, "If you come back tonight and bring your family to the talk, there will be something very special waiting for you. However, you have to bring your gift cards and your family."

The talk began that evening. There were about six hundred people in attendance. I scanned the audience and didn't see the boy or his family. Then, about five minutes past six o'clock, he walked in. Near the end of the presentation, I said, "Where is the kid that I told, 'if you come tonight, you will receive something special'?"

He raised his hand, sitting in the last pew beside his family. He came forward, and I asked him to step up to the ambo and then asked him to share what happened earlier in the day. He shared the story.

I asked him, "Did you get the answer right?"

He said, "Yes, Father."

"No, not at first you didn't." I corrected, and people laughed.

He then explained the situation to everyone in attendance.

I said, "There's something special about you. I don't know what it is, but there is. I told you that something special would happen to you if you came tonight with your family and brought your gift cards. Did I not?"

He said, "Yes, Father."

"Do you have your gift cards?" I asked. He did, and I said, "Give them to me. Today you lose your gift cards, but today, you gain a one-year scholarship to the De La Salle High School."

He smiled widely, and people applauded the young man. Then I gave him his gift cards back. (His picture is in the Image Gallery.)

The whole point of that story is that God always involves others in any type of miracle. In other words, God never acts alone. For the miracles to be made manifest, He works through us. His miracles don't only happen *to* us, they happen *through* us. Which means, we have to do our part. We have to make an effort.

Have you heard the story of the crippled man by the pool of Siloam? Jesus noticed a lame man begging to get into the pool.

Jesus asked the man, "Why aren't you getting in the pool?"

To which the man replied, "Because no one will help me get into the pool. When the pool gets stirred up, I need someone to help me." (That was when the healing was said to take place.)

Jesus said, "You're healed because of your belief. Pick up your mat and go."

The man was instantly healed. He stood, picked up his mat, and went home.

Yes, Jesus spoke the words that incited the man's healing. However, Jesus required that the man also take action. Jesus didn't carry him into the pool or help him wade in the stirred water. Jesus called upon him to act. He called upon him to answer the call. So the man did. He picked up his mat and went—forever healed.

The same happened with the miracle of Lazarus. Lazarus had been dead for four days in the tomb. Jesus went to the tomb, and

He wept for Lazarus. He was moved with emotion, and He asked others to roll the stone away from the tomb. Did Jesus go inside the tomb and get Lazarus? No. What did Jesus do? Jesus said, "Lazarus, come out!" Remember, Lazarus had been dead for four days, wrapped and bound. But Lazarus got up, hobbled out, was unbound, and lived.

The lesson that I felt called to share that night with the young boy is that he had to make an effort. He was willing to risk. He held his hand in the air to be called upon, even though his teacher signaled to him that he shouldn't even try. That day, he realized that he could trust, and he could take risks. Even though he didn't know the answer, with the help of another he was able to figure it out.

Over three hundred and sixty-five times in scripture, God tells us, "Be not afraid." That's very interesting because there are three hundred and sixty-five days a year. We're told each day, "Be not afraid." We are reminded that God is with us. But we can't just be sitting on our butts waiting for God to do all the work. We have to step forward. Just as Lazarus answered the call of Jesus and stepped forward to be awakened and return to life. We are being called similarly. We are being called to try. God will help you, but you have to put in the effort. So, if you plan to move mountains, you better put on your overalls, pick up your shovel, and start digging.

Frequent Flyer

According to Delta Air Lines, if you average it out, I'm on a plane three hundred and fifty days a year. As one who travels so often, you need to know that I only bring one suitcase with me. I bring my clerics and what I wear on an airplane—my shorts, my hoodie, my sandals—and that's it. And let me tell you something, when you board an aircraft dressed as a priest, amazing things happen. You'd think Moses was parting the Red Sea the way people turn to look and start talking. I walk onto the plane in my collar, and this is what I hear, "Oh, honey, thank God. There's a priest on our flight."

I think to myself, *They wouldn't be thanking God if they knew my driving record.*

People do the most bizarre things. They'll knock over their drink. They hide their *Vogue* magazine. They start talking about religion, which they know nothing about. They sit up straight, and I walk by and say, "I'm not a nun, okay? Relax."

To avoid that whole rigmarole, I wear my shorts, my sandals, and my hoodie. I always get a window seat, settle in, put up my hoodie, and go to sleep.

Not too long ago, I was flying to Melbourne, Australia. I flew from Lexington to Atlanta. Atlanta to Los Angeles. Then on the same day, I was scheduled to fly with Virgin Australia from Los Angeles nonstop to Melbourne. The last leg of the trip was sixteen hours, nonstop. When I got to the international terminal at the airport in Los Angeles, I went up to the gate, and the screen said, *Melbourne, Australia—Canceled.*

I don't know if you know this, but if you fly to Australia on a Thursday, you don't get there until Saturday. But if you leave on Saturday from Melbourne, Australia, you get to Los Angeles on Saturday. It makes no sense!

I asked the gate agent, "When is the next flight to Melbourne?"

They said, "On Monday."

I said, "That would mean I'll get there on Wednesday. I'm scheduled to speak Saturday through Tuesday."

So what did I do? Naturally, I threw a fit!

They said, "Calm down. Calm down. We'll get you on a flight." And they did. They put me on a Qantas flight. Qantas is the national airline for Australia.

Thank God, I was given a window seat.

I boarded the plane, sat down, put up my hoodie, and I fell asleep. I woke up so refreshed. I felt so renewed. I looked at the monitor, and it said fourteen more hours to go. You know what I did? I pulled out my rosary that I carry with me, and I started praying the rosary. Then, guess what happened. The unthinkable on a plane.

Tap. Tap. Tap.

I'm thinking, *I know the person sitting next to me has not just tapped me.*

Another rule in airplane etiquette: don't make eye contact—with anyone. Because once you make eye contact with people, guess what? You're engaged with that person. So even though I thought I felt a tap, the last thing I wanted to do was make eye contact. And then there it was again.

Tap. Tap.

I turned and looked at the woman while praying my rosary, and she said, "Excuse me. Are you praying?"

I held up my rosary, like, *Uh, hello?*

I broke eye contact and went back to praying my rosary. Then there it was again!

Tap. Tap. Tap.

God give me patience . . . *Hail Mary, full of grace. The Lord be with thee.* She tapped again. I looked at her and said, "Can I help you?"

She said, and I quote, "Would you pray for me?"

I said, "Yes, ma'am. I'll pray for you." Then I returned to my rosary. *Hail Mary, full of grace.*

Tap. Tap.

"Yes, ma'am?" I asked. And said, "I'm not going to be able to pray for you if we keep talking like this."

She said, "Well, I want to tell you why I need you to pray for me." She then proceeded to tell me, "I'm on my second diagnosis of stage four breast cancer. For the second time. I also have a tumor on my sacrum."

And here I was, I had been such a jerk! I looked at her and said, "Of course, I'll pray for you. In fact, I'm going to pray right now for God's healing upon you." I told her, "My name is Father Jim. I'm a Papal Missionary for Pope Francis."

With me, I carry these little crosses that the pope gave me. I reached out to her, took her hand, and placed one of the pope's crosses in her palm. I said, "Be assured of God's prayer and God's healing for you."

She burst into tears. She said, "Thank you. My name is Olivia Newton-John."

I looked at her quizzically and did my best impression of her role from the film *Grease*, singing, "You're the one that I want. Woo. Woo. Woo." She looked at me seriously, and I asked her, "Like, that one?"

She said, "Yes."

Olivia Newton-John is not Catholic. She and I parted ways at the Melbourne, Australia, airport. That evening, I gave my first presentation at St. Agatha's Parish in Cranbourne, Australia. Who walked through the doors at St. Agatha's Catholic Church for the 5:00 p.m. Mass? Olivia Newton-John and her husband, John Easterling. Who showed up for the 8:00 a.m. Mass and the 10:00 a.m. Mass? Olivia Newton-John and her husband, John Easterling. Where did I find them after each Mass? Not out greeting the thousands of fans—and I mean thousands literally (you think she's a star in the United States; you should see what she is in her homeland when word gets out in Cranbourne). No, where did I find her and her husband? Kneeling before the Blessed Sacrament.

How did I know where they were? Because I was on the side, waiting for our selfie. Hey, I'm just being honest. And wouldn't you know it, around her neck, the very next day after we met, she wore the cross from Pope Francis. (You can see our picture in the Image Gallery.)

What I'm saying is, you don't have to be a jerk. And when you realize you are, you take responsibility and accountability for your behavior. You apologize. You say you're sorry, and you allow God's grace to blossom. You see, my brothers and sisters, I'm not perfect, but I try my best. I do what I can to allow God to use me as an instrument for His will, which I currently believe is to inspire others to more deeply love the Lord, one another, and themselves. That's why I share stories and travel to share the Good News.

When I travel throughout the world, speaking or presenting, people need to realize that these events are not assigned to me. By my bishop's blessing, and actually by my bishop's design, for which I am grateful, I am allowed to travel and preach in ways that would ordinarily be impossible for a diocesan priest such as myself. However, my bishop does not assign where I will be and when. All the speaking events occur through invitation and by word of mouth. If I have an opening and receive an invitation, I place myself there. It has always been my belief that when the invitations cease, that will be God's way of directing me to where my next chapter will begin. For now, I answer the call that I feel God is presenting in my life, wherever that may be. For example, I recently received an invitation to speak in Biloxi, Mississippi, in January. After that, another invitation arrived to speak in Omaha, Nebraska, in 2023.

The current way in which God calls me to serve reminds me of lyrics from a beloved Johnny Cash song that goes, "Children go where I send thee. How shall I send thee? I'm going to send thee two by two. Two by Paul and Silas, and one by the little biddy baby who was born, born, born in Bethlehem. . . ."

Meaning, God knows exactly where I need to be at precisely the right time at the right place. For instance, I spoke at a parish during the pandemic. The parish had not been allowed to attend

Mass for months. The #60MinutesforJesus event was their first time back in church. Who would have known this? But God did. God placed me there to provide that which the parish needed, and at that moment, the parish seemed to need encouragement, laughter, and reflection. To be a vessel for God in such a way relates to what Pope Francis calls the Ministry of Presence. To really be present with one another, we must tune in, slow down, and be there, sharing in the moment with whomever we are with.

One of the reasons I arrive a day early for speaking events is to attend liturgies there at the church and visit within the local community so that I can get a feel of the people who will be in attendance. Even though I don't have a local flock, there's nothing worse than a priest who is not a shepherd to His people. God places me there for a short time to challenge, to motivate, to affirm, and then for them to carry on that which they have learned in our short time together while I hop on to somewhere else. I see myself and the #60MinutesforJesus mission like a booster shot in the arms of the faithful while we are together. Then, after I leave, the actual task begins as they sit with the lessons, the challenges, or the affirmations and implement that which has been learned.

As anyone who knows me can attest, I'm not perfect, far from it even. However, even in my imperfection, God can still make use of me for His will. But that's one of the exceptional aspects of building a relationship with God—we don't have to be perfect. The truth is, I don't need to be perfect to inspire others. Neither do you. We don't need to be saints to allow God to work through us and use us to inspire others, help others, uplift one another. We can all do this. I try to inspire others by sharing how I deal with my own imperfections, hoping that others may recognize that despite our brokenness, despite our sinfulness, despite our moments of pridefulness and weakness, God still loves us just the same. None of us are perfect. Yet, in how we deal with our imperfections, we can allow those aspects of ourselves to serve as teaching moments for others. That's what I try to do. And I say, "It's better to live your life knowing that you're not perfect than spending your whole life pretending to be."

We're all broken vessels. It is through our imperfections and through the cracks where God most brilliantly shines through in our lives. This metaphor is expressed beautifully through the ancient Japanese tradition of kintsugi, the art of putting broken pottery pieces back together with gold—a metaphor for embracing our flaws and imperfections.

Rather than attempting to conceal the flaws in the pottery, kintsugi embraces the imperfection, crafting new and beautifully unique designs around each "flaw." Similarly, we often try to hide our own imperfections within our lives. We hide what doesn't feel perfect within us, what we know to be sinful or kept secret, for fear, questioning whether that imperfection is lovable. In our embarrassment or our shame, we attempt to conceal the crack. We worry whether *we* are lovable in the wholeness of who we are, in the fullness of our being. The love of God, my brothers and sisters, is that gold, capable of mending our flaws and making us whole again. When we embrace the love of God, we allow the light to shine through the cracks within our broken vessels. Each of us is a unique, one-of-a-kind work of art, molded by God's hand. You see, we don't have to be perfect because we are already perfectly imperfect in the eyes of God.

When asking ourselves what it means to love, I think a little girl named Emma K., age six, nailed it when she wrote, "What is love? Love is when you're missing some of your teeth, but you're not afraid to smile because you know your friends will still love you even though some of you is missing."

When it comes to being our full, authentic selves, just be you, and if people don't like it, then find new people.

Not everyone will love us for exactly who we are, and you know what? That's okay. That's *their* issue, not yours. Christ loves us unconditionally, regardless of our imperfections. He sees our flaws, yet His love for us never falters, despite the cracks in our broken vessels, and, yes, even if we happen to be missing a tooth or two.

Family Time

One year, several days before Christmas, I spoke in England for a #60MinutesforJesus event. I planned to stay in England until my return flight home several days later, on Christmas Eve. I received a phone call from my mother after my talk on the twentieth. She said, "Jimmy."

I said, "Yes, ma'am?"

She said, "This is your mother."

I said, "Yes, ma'am. I know that."

She said, "I need you to be home tomorrow. We're having a family meeting. I've called all your brothers and sisters." Remember, I'm the youngest of five children. My brothers, sisters, and I live all across the United States. She said, "I've called all your brothers and sisters, and they're coming home tomorrow. I need you here."

I said, "Mother, I'm sorry. I'm overseas in a country called England. I won't be able to be there."

She said, "Jimmy, I'm your mother. I'll see you tomorrow." Then she hung up the phone! That's my mother for you.

So what did I do? I did as she asked. I canceled the last two days of my talk. I called British Airways and they agreed to change my ticket. Before long, I was flying from London, England, nonstop to Houston, Texas. I then rented a car and drove to Orange, Texas, where I met my brothers and sisters. My mom, the matriarch, sat in her chair, four-feet-eight-inches tall, eighty-five years old, in the center of us all.

She said to us, "I've been thinking. We need to bond as a family."

I thought, *What? She dragged us all here for* this?

She continued, "So, I have registered all of us to take a CPR class at the American Red Cross on Pine Avenue."

I said, "Are you serious? I flew all the way from London, England, to Houston, Texas, to take a CPR class with my brothers and sisters, and you, Mother, so we can all *bond*?"

The next thing I knew, I was performing chest compressions on one of those dummies, reciting, "One, one thousand. Two, one thousand. Three, one thousand."

We passed the class. We all received CPR certification that day. Then we went to celebrate as a family. As Italians, what do you think we did to celebrate? We ate! That's what Italians do!

When deciding where to eat, my mother came up with another idea for us all. She said, "Let's feed two birds with one crumb. Let's go to the mall where we can finish our Christmas shopping, and we can eat there."

Have you ever been to a mall on December 21? Let me just tell you this—don't.

We got there, and we walked together, weaving through the

crowds, me beside my four-foot-eight Italian mother alongside my brothers and sisters. We ordered food and sat together, eating in the mall's food court. Suddenly, my mother looked alarmed. She spotted a man lying on the floor in the middle of the food court with people surrounding him. My mother didn't hesitate for an instant. She jumped from her seat and ran toward the crowd faster than you've ever seen a little Italian woman run, screaming, "I have just been certified in CPR! I have just been certified in CPR!"

She broke through the crowd, landed on top of the man on the floor, and began chest compressions. The police officers lifted her away from the man and said, "Excuse us, ma'am. We're trying to arrest this man for shoplifting."

Strangely enough, the officer who arrested the man went to high school with me, Lannie Claybar. Lannie said, "Wait, is that Father Jim's mom?"

I looked the other way, like, "Nope. Not today. Definitely not my mother. No relation."

That's just how my mother is. But you see, I understand that about my mother because I spend time with her. She acted with love first and took a leap. I understand she operates that way. Catholics and Christians, let me tell you something. If your Bible is in good shape, you aren't. Think about it. To know God and to know the voice of God in our lives, we have to spend time with God; in prayer, in our thoughts, in our actions, reading the scripture. How else can we know how He operates? If we begin to understand God and develop a relationship with Him, we recognize that we must not only read the Word of God, but we must also obey the Word of God. Let's face it—God gave us the Ten Commandments, not the Ten Suggestions. Think about it, people.

When you spend time with God and form that relationship, we are then called to surrender to God's will. That's a big one, especially for people in the United States—surrendering. All too often, we're afraid to let go. We think we know what's best, when really, we may only be seeing a tiny slice of the whole pie, just like my mother. She leaped with the purest of intentions, only to later realize that she didn't know the entire picture. We often think we're God and try to take control of a situation. We're not God. But God dwells within us, and us within Him. To recognize that, we must set aside our egos and realize that we are not almighty. We are human; therefore, we are fallible. We trip and fall, and we make mistakes. We are lovable and loved by God all the same, perfect in our imperfection.

Even the most notable characters of the Bible were just as imperfect as we are today. Did you know that Moses stuttered? Gideon was a coward. Samson, with his long hair, was a womanizer. Ahab married a prostitute. Jeremiah and Timothy were too young. David was an adulterer and a murderer. Elijah was suicidal. Isaiah preached naked—God forbid. Jonah ran from God. Naomi, a widow. Job, bankrupt. John the Baptist ate bugs! Peter denied Christ. The disciples fell asleep while praying. Martha worried about everything. The Samaritan woman divorced more than once. Zacchaeus was too small. Timothy suffered an ulcer. Paul, too religious. Lazarus . . . dead!

Let me share something with you. You're not the Message. But if you let God in, you can be the messenger.

Miss Marie's Spaghetti Sauce

I was a mama's boy, the youngest of five children. My mother came from Cosenza, Italy. She was Calabrese, meaning she was from a town in southern Italy near the coast of the Tyrrhenian Sea. She was four feet, eight inches tall. Her name was Maria Ceraso Sichko, born on the Assumption of Mary. My mother, God rest her soul, was an amazing woman. She taught us at a very young age that everything you do, you give.

My earliest memory of my mother is from the age of four years old. I remember waking up early one morning on a Tuesday to her in the kitchen cooking. I remember watching her prepare her pasta, homemade noodles, her special sauce, and everything that goes with it to make a full Italian meal. (For those who know how Italians eat, you know it's a big production.) She then set the dining room table with our best china and silver. At eleven o'clock, who walked through the front door? Four huge, stinky, smelly sanitation workers, African American sanitation workers.

Where did they go? They sat down in the dining room that had been prepared for them.

My mother taught all her children, "You serve those men because they serve you." It doesn't matter if they look different or even if they smell. Can I tell you something? My family was probably the only family in the history of the world that planned their weeks around Tuesday, eleven o'clock, trash day.

In 2017, on Tuesday, January 24, I happened to be preaching in Texas. I decided to drive to visit my eighty-eight-year-old mother. As usual, I found her in the kitchen, busy making everything, as she always did on Tuesdays. At eleven o'clock, in walked the trash collectors, per usual, and they sat gathered at the dining room table.

My mother fed these guys on January 24, at eleven in the morning, and then after they ate, I walked outside to take the picture with them. (There's a picture with the sanitation workers that day in the Image Gallery.) I walked back inside, and my mother had collapsed. She died in hospice shortly thereafter.

I was devastated, and I'm still devastated to this day.

My mother left only five things in her will for the children. Everything else had to be given away to the poor. Each of her children got one thing. My oldest brother got the Nativity set. My mother gave me her sauce recipe—a note in my mother's handwriting on a single piece of paper, and no one's getting it from me. All my brothers and sisters want it. Too bad because they ain't getting it! It stays with me and travels with me everywhere I go. Her handwritten recipe is a memento from my mother that I will forever cherish.

Everyone my mother cooked for just loved her cooking, and

for her, it was a way to feed others and to show her love through the dishes she prepared. The "secret sauce" of her cooking, quite literally, was her sauce! She always made her sauce from scratch, and it was always the focal point of her meals, especially her dinners.

Before my mother passed away, I had intended to have a batch of her sauce made and bottled to give away to her closest family and friends on her ninetieth birthday in August of 2018. My mother passed away at eighty-eight years old, and I didn't get the chance to share her sauce in the way I dreamed.

In memory of my mother, I sent the sauce recipe to my good friend Chef Giada De Laurentiis to ask her thoughts. Have you heard of her? If not, don't worry. We took a selfie. (It's in the Image Gallery.) Giada taste-tested the sauce because it's all-natural and made with no preservatives, and she said, "You've got to bottle this."

I told her, "I'm thinking of bottling a few batches to give away at my mother's ninetieth birthday for her lady friends."

She said, "No, you need to bottle this."

I had no idea what I was doing, but I considered her sugges-tion as a way for my mother's legacy to live on. So I decided to bottle her recipe. Looking back, I now recognize that it is entirely unheard of for a food or beverage product to go from inception, through federal approvals, through distribution, to release and onto store shelves so quickly, but that is precisely what happened. My mother died on January 25, 2017, and her sauce was released on August 15, 2018. To be honest, the plan to bottle her sauce wasn't set in motion until several months after January 25, so it speaks even more to the role that God played in bringing her sauce to fruition.

Mind you, my God-given skill set is not in the nitty-gritty. When the inspiration to bottle my mom's sauce was brought up, I thought, *Okay, I just need to have her sauce cooked and then bottle it. Simple!*

I reached out to friends who had knowledge in the industry, Alissa Lundergan, Chef Ouita Michel, Chef Giada, Nancy Ward. All these wonderful, knowledgeable people—none of them turned me down in my desire to bottle my mom's sauce, but they directed me to others whom they suggested I needed to know. When I told each of them that I wanted the sauce to be released by August 15, 2018, they found this funny. At the time, I didn't understand why. Turns out, it is a huge process! One that usually takes years.

I started the process by taking their advice. I called a gentleman, a food manufacturer, and asked him, "Can you make one hundred bottles of my mom's sauce? I'd like to give them away in honor of my mother."

The man said to me, "There is no way that this can be achieved."

Basically, he said, "Thanks, but no thanks." Then he hung up on me. It was no more than a five-minute call. For anyone who has ever been politely dismissed, you know the kind of call I'm talking about.

When you're a dreamer, as I am, and you truly believe in what you're called to do, you learn not to take no as your final answer. Just consider my vocation story and journey being ordained into the priesthood: I was first denied by a diocese right at the last minute before I was to be ordained; when I chose to continue the process in the hopes of becoming ordained, people asked me, "Why would you want to be a priest when your own church and brother priests are basically saying, 'We don't want you?' Why would you want that?"

Such moments in life can cause us to ask ourselves, *Is this my true calling?* Often though, it's more on the surface because when you know what you're called to do, you do it. Regardless of obstacles, you continue. That's when trusting in God comes into play. It doesn't mean that whatever you strive to do will be accomplished. However, it does mean that you must put in the effort to the best of your ability if the impossible is to become possible. Nothing is impossible with God. God can use the impossibilities that we see to create something possible if only we meet Him halfway and see it through with our efforts.

So, after I was initially dismissed, I went back to my chef friends and told them what happened. They said, "Don't give it away. If you make the sauce, you don't want to do that. This stuff is great! You should make it available for purchase."

That's when the idea came about to donate the proceeds. If I was going to sell Mom's sauce, then I wanted to give proceeds to two important organizations that touched not only our family's lives or the lives of other families but specifically organizations that touched my mother's life. The first was the Catholic Diocese of Lexington, and their mission to help the most impoverished people in Eastern Kentucky and the Appalachian Mountains. The second was Southeast Texas Hospice, the first hospice in Texas and one of the first ten hospice organizations in the United States. Southeast Texas Hospice is not only a place where the sick and elderly die; the staff also minister to those who are in the process of dying and comfort them as they are there with them, and for them, through their final days. They bring hope to the dying and their families. The organization was only a part of my mother's journey for a matter of hours, but the impact they made on her, and me, was monumental.

I didn't give up. I knew that I wanted to still pursue the impossible. Out of the blue, miraculously, the food manufacturer who had initially dismissed me called me back. He said, "I may know someone who would be willing to take this on. You should call David Ochoa of Bluegrass Superior foods."

I called David immediately. I told him about my vision to make the sauce a reality, and he said, "Yeah, we'll do it."

Just like that!

Then we began the process. It was a long process. We had to jump through all the hoops required by the government and the FDA. We came up with the barcodes and the labeling, and everything had to be on the label in specific fonts and in particular ways. I'm serious. Over three hundred pages from the Food and Drug Administration described what had to be on the label and why. The font, the image, the nutritional values, it all had to be to their standards. Then we had to get a license to sell a food product, and then guess what? We had to have insurance. What about the container? We had to decide whether the sauce would be in a bottle or in a jar. Would it have a screw-on lid? Would it have wax? How could we guarantee that it would be adequately sealed? There were so many moving parts that went into what first seemed like a simple idea. Then we had to go through the taste-test samples and figure out manufacturing, distribution, shipping, refrigeration, and where it would be stored. It went on and on. I didn't know about all that . . . I'm a priest!

I thought, *Good Lord! What have I gotten myself into?*

But here's the thing. God found a way. Philippians 4:13 says, "I can do all things through Christ who strengthens me." Yes, but it's like the time my brothers invited me to attend a boxing match. We sat ringside, and both fighters, Oscar De La Hoya and Floyd Mayweather entered the ring. As De La Hoya raised his arms and began to dance, he saw my collar and caught my eyes. Everyone watched as he made his way over to me and leaned over the ropes. I glanced up at the Jumbotron to see me and the legendary boxer in large, bright colors on the massive display.

The fighter marked himself with the sign of the cross, kissed his gloves, then saluted me. I gave him a little wave and said a blessing. The crowd roared with excitement.

My brother leaned over to me and asked, "Jimmy, will that help him win the match?"

I offered a half smile. "Sure . . . if he knows how to box!"

The same goes for Miss Marie's Spaghetti Sauce. We put in the effort, and God made the impossible possible. It amazed me how everything came together. We were so efficient that we launched within an amazingly short time period, in time for my mother's birthday on August 15, 2018. And another aspect that made the process all the more challenging was that none of my brothers or sisters knew about it. No one that I would be sharing the sauce with on my mother's birthday knew because I wanted it to be a surprise. In fact, I didn't even tell my bishop about it, even though half the proceeds would be going to the diocese.

I'll never forget the day I decided on the final packaging of the sauce. I mailed a package to my bishop and asked him not to open the box until I arrived. He waited until I met him at his office. We sat down, and he opened the package. He said, "Did you bottle your mother's salad dressing?" (I don't know why he thought that, but he did.)

I said, "No, look." Then he saw I bottled my mother's

spaghetti sauce with partial proceeds going to the diocese. He was instantly supportive and excited that I was carrying on my mother's tradition through her sauce.

On my mother's birthday, I had Miss Marie's Spaghetti Sauce sent to each of my brothers and sisters as a surprise. They loved it. They did say it's nearly impossible to replicate our mother's sauce exactly as she prepared it. Still, my siblings all believe it's 95 to 98 percent exact to the way they remember our mom's sauce. Soon after that, we had an unveiling. Her sauce is now being sold across the country. It is being sold in grocery stores and being served at restaurants and on people's dinner tables. It's amazing for me to see all the pictures that people send to me or tag me in on social media. People will say, "We're using your mother's sauce tonight for family pizza night." Or they say, "We're using your mother's sauce as a parish fundraiser. We're making a big spaghetti dinner." Or people say, "We're using your mother's sauce in our Bloody Marys." (You can see some of the photos in the Image Gallery.)

It's so touching to see other families carrying on my mom's tradition, making their family dinner all over the world, and coming up with unique ways to incorporate her sauce in their own recipes and family gatherings. The moments are exactly what my mother would have loved. For an Italian mother, feeding those she loves was important. She loved and prayed for us all, tirelessly. Eating, and especially eating together, is vital in an Italian family. Food brings us together. We see this all the way back to Jesus feeding His followers. It is beautiful to see how that sacrament is being accomplished through her sauce. My mother's presence continues, and it feels as though she is alive, in a different way. She is still present, in a unique way now.

Her tradition of giving and receiving, which she instilled in her children, continues.

The scripture says death is not the end. First Corinthians 15:55–57 says, "O death, where is thy sting? O grave, where is thy victory?" Some people consider death the end. For Christians, it is just the beginning of eternal life. Though my mother's physical presence is no longer with us, her presence has become multiplied. People have come to know her who otherwise would never have encountered her. If my mother were alive today to see the impact of her sauce, I think she would be incredibly proud and shocked about how it's taken off. As of this writing, we've sold over fifty thousand bottles and recently hit a milestone of over one hundred thousand dollars given to charity.

If I had listened to that first food manufacturer, none of it would have happened. And even more interesting, that same food manufacturer now distributes Miss Marie's Spaghetti Sauce!

That's how the Holy Spirit works. God opened the doors and brought individuals along my path to help bring Miss Marie's to life, but we had to roll up our sleeves and get to work! The Holy Spirit will pave the way and through Him we can do all things— if we're willing to put in the effort.

Random Acts of Kindness

Whenever I fly, I always, always, *always* bring the flight attendants coffee, or sometimes gift cards, chocolates, or handwritten notes of encouraging words so that they know the passengers appreciate them and their service. That's how I was raised. My mother taught my siblings and me to always show appreciation for those who serve us. It's only a small act of kindness to show my gratitude to the airline workers, but even such a simple gesture of appreciation can make someone's day. We never know what struggles someone else may be going through in their day, so any opportunity we get to lighten another's load and maybe even bring a smile to their face, I say, why not?

When is it a good time to be kind? *Always.*

When you win, be kind.

When you are ignored, be kind.

When you are stuck, be kind.

When you are upset, be kind.

When you are disappointed, be kind.

When you are in doubt, be kind.

When you are scared, be kind.

Being kind is not a sign of weakness. Kindness will always serve you well. #bekind.

It's like the encounter I had with Delta Air Lines. I was traveling, per usual, flying from Houston to Lexington through Atlanta, and I gave gift cards to the flight attendants to say thank you for their service. I took selfies with the staff holding their gift cards, and then I tweeted the picture. Delta retweeted the photo and messaged me, saying, "We see you have an hour and a half layover. Could we meet you for a conversation?"

When I got off the plane, representatives from Delta met me at the gate. They escorted me to the Sky Club and asked if they could film me. I didn't mind. I said, "Sure."

Right then and there, they brought cameras and a film crew into the room and interviewed me. They asked about my experiences with Delta and why I bring gifts for the staff. I told them about how much I appreciate the staff and how for someone like me who travels so often, the airline staff, in a way, becomes like a family. They greet me with kindness along my travels and make sure I arrive safely to my destinations. Giving gifts is simply a way for me to express gratitude and repay their kindness.

After the interview, they escorted me to my connecting flight, and off I went.

Little did I know, they filmed an entire commercial that day! (There's a screenshot of the commercial in the Image Gallery.)

All that began from a simple act of kindness. The CEO of Delta, Ed Bastian, even reached out to me after that to say thank you and invited me to the Delta headquarters on May 20. We met and shared a wonderful conversation, and I gave him one of the crosses blessed by Pope Francis. He emailed shortly after that and wrote, "Fr. Jim—wow is my reaction as well. It was a special visit, and I already feel a kinship with you. Thank you for the special blessing from our Holy Father. I am already looking for the best place to display it in my home. So thoughtful. But thank you especially for sharing your heart and message with our team and me. I want you to be a regular guest. You inspire a servant heart that I want to infuse in all our people. Please send me the plans for your next visit to Rome with your colleagues. We will take care of them. Also, I will put you in touch with our head of catering to see how they can evaluate your sauce. Safe travels, my friend. I look forward to seeing you soon. Ed."

Kindness begets more kindness. Gratitude, appreciation, and taking a moment to say thank you and #bekind will always serve you. A. A. Milne, the author of the beloved *Winnie-the-Pooh* children's books, wrote, "Piglet noticed that even though he had a very small heart, it could hold a rather large amount of gratitude."

Shortly thereafter, Delta's chief health officer, Dr. Henry Ting, reached out by email and wrote, ". . . Given the immense mental stress, social divisions, and anger many people are experiencing, your real experiences of mercy and random acts of kindness are both inspiring and promote joy. We are developing our flight plan for wellness and well-being, and I believe there are opportunities for us to partner. Let's visit soon. Best, Henry."

In Matthew 17:20, Jesus says, ". . . Truly I tell you, if you have faith like a grain of mustard seed, you can say to this mountain, 'Move from here to there,' and it will move. Nothing will be impossible for you."

Our faith, no matter how large or small, is put into motion through our actions. When we act with kindness, God acknowledges our faith and works alongside us, facilitating miracles far beyond our imaginings for the greater good. As Jesus says, "If you have faith . . . Nothing will be impossible for you," the same is true for acts of mercy. Acts of gratitude. Acts of appreciation and thanks. The sixth-century philosopher Aesop said, "No act of kindness, no matter how small, is ever wasted." The truth is, there's no such thing as a small act of kindness. Every act creates a ripple with no logical end . . .

I wonder, what can God accomplish through us all when we put our faith into action?

Delta Downs

There have been many times when I've offered to pay for someone or something and let's face it, I don't even have the money to do it! But when the time comes, God provides. Here's my usual travel schedule, nearly every week; I fly on Saturday, speak until Wednesday, and return home Thursday afternoon. In that brief window, when I'm home, I pick up my dog, Gracie Marie, who stays out on a farm while I travel. I pick up my mail and sort through it. I'll catch up on household chores that need tending to, like my laundry. I connect with my bishop. I return my dog back out to the farm, and then I pack my bag for my upcoming flight. That's my routine. And, of course, throughout that time, I pray.

The night before a scheduled flight, I always look through a stack of folders beside my bed before I go to sleep. Traveling so often, I can't keep track of it all without the help of these folders that tell me where I'm going. While I look through the itinerary,

I always google where I'm going. This helps me prepare for where I will speak and familiarize myself with the area.

One night, I googled the place where I was scheduled to speak, and the first thing that popped up was my face! Next to my picture, it said, "Come listen to Father Jim Sichko, Papal Missionary of Mercy, $75 per ticket."

When I read this, I was shocked for several reasons. The first being that I wouldn't listen to myself for seventy-five dollars a ticket! I wouldn't! On top of that, I clearly state in my speaking arrangements that I don't allow people to charge admission to hear me speak. I didn't know what to do. I flew down there the next day, on Saturday as scheduled. I said to the priest there, "What are you doing? Why are you charging people to hear me speak?"

He said, "Because, Father, you're our remaining fundraiser for this year. We're hoping to reach our goal."

I asked, "What are you raising money for?"

They said, "We're building a garden in honor of our Blessed Mother. Right now, we're five thousand dollars short."

You know what I did, don't you?

I told them to give the money back to all the people who purchased tickets, and I wrote them a check for $5,000. That didn't mean I had $5,000 in the account. But guess what? They didn't know that. It wasn't going to be until Monday or Tuesday until they tried to cash the check. By then, I'd be gone!

Kidding, of course, but seriously, I wasn't worried. God provides.

It was a three-night talk. Between fifteen hundred and two thousand people showed up the first night. One thing you've probably gathered about me thus far is that I'm spontaneous. After speaking the first night, I drove two and a half hours on

Interstate 10 to my mother's house. She didn't know I was coming. I arrived around 11:00 that night and went to sleep.

She woke me up early the following day, excited that I was home. I told her, "Mother, you know I'm speaking two and a half hours away, but until one o'clock, we'll do whatever you want to do today."

My mother said, "Let's go to Delta Downs. They have a wonderful buffet." She was eighty-six at the time, and she told me, "But let's get there early before the old people get there."

If you don't know what Delta Downs is, it's a casino. And my mother was right. They do have a fantastic buffet. If you've never been there or never been to a casino, I'll tell you now, the people who design these casinos are not stupid. They put the buffets in the back of the casinos. That way, you have to walk through the gambling areas if you want to eat.

Here I was walking through the casino in my clerics with my eighty-six-year-old, four-foot-eight Italian mother. My mother would always say to me, "Slow down. You are walking too fast for me."

I told her, "Mom, we're trying to get to the buffet before the old people get there."

We took a break, and she stopped to catch her breath. Something my mother always did was put a one-dollar bill in my pocket. I don't know why, but she did that my entire life. I always assumed it was in case I needed to make a phone call or in case of an emergency.

While waiting for her to catch her breath, I took out the one-dollar bill and put it in the Triple Sizzlin' 7 penny slot machine. I hit the button. Lights flashed, and then the sirens went off. I hit the jackpot. How much was the jackpot?

$5,000.

Out they came with that big ol' check. You know those giant cardboard checks? That's what it was. It said, "Pay to the order of Father Jim Sichko. From Delta Downs casino."

My mother nudged me quietly and said, "Jimmy, let's go home. We're going to get robbed carrying that thing around."

I was like, "No, let's go to the buffet!"

But she insisted, so we left. We went home. Then I returned to the speaking engagement that evening. What do you think I brought with me? That's right. That big ol' check. I held up the check, and I said, "Do you see, people? When you give, you always receive. God always provides."

He does. That doesn't mean that you're not going to suffer. That doesn't mean that you're not going to have pains. That doesn't mean that you're not going to wander and question. What it does mean is that God ultimately provides—always. Why will He always provide for us? Because He created us. Because we are a part of Him.

He says, "I formed you. I knew you before you were born. I can count the number of hairs on your head . . ." (or for some of us, the lack thereof.) God will never, ever forsake us.

In Isaiah 43:1–3, the scripture reminds us, "But now thus says the Lord, He who created you, O Jacob, He who formed you, O Israel, 'Fear not, for I have redeemed you; I have called you by name, you are mine. When you pass through the waters, I will be with you; and through the rivers, they shall not overwhelm you; when you walk through fire, you shall not be burned, and the flame shall not consume you. For I am the Lord your God, the Holy One of Israel, your Savior.'"

Names are important. When someone calls you by name, it

means they know you. God reminds us that we are known to Him throughout the scripture and that He supports us. Exodus 14:14 says, "The Lord will fight for you, and you have only to be still." We stand up for those who we believe in. That is what God is saying in this scripture. He's saying, "I believe in you." And in other words, he's saying, "Relax. I've got your back." In Psalm 139:17, God reminds us that he thinks of us. The scripture reads, "How precious to me are thy thoughts, O God! How vast is the sum of them!" We're constantly in the presence of God. Not only do we dwell within God, but God, too, dwells within us. We are one with Him.

Jeremiah 29:11 says, "For I know the plans I have for you, says the Lord, plans for welfare and not for evil, to give you a future and a hope." They are not necessarily my plans, and they're not necessarily your plans. But when we put our faith in God and trust that God will provide, God, in fact, provides. He always does.

Psalm 62:5–8 says, "For God alone, my soul waits in silence, for my hope is from Him. He only is my rock and my salvation, my fortress; I shall not be shaken. On God rests my deliverance and my honor; my mighty rock, my refuge is God. Trust in Him at all times, O people; pour out your heart before Him; God is a refuge for us."

God is our refuge. He will provide for us. Not necessarily what we *want*, but He will provide what we *need*. Our needs and our wants are two entirely different things. It is up to us to recognize this and align our wants with God's needs for us.

Though we may feel abandoned or lost at times or even carry the burden of the cross at times, God never leaves us. As Pope Francis says, "There is no cross, big or small in our life which the

Lord does not share with us." If anything, we are the ones who abandon God.

Just as described in the beloved poem "Footprints" by Margaret Fishback Powers, there will be two sets of footprints in the earth beneath our feet when we choose to walk with the Lord. One set of prints will be ours, and the other set belongs to the Lord, walking by our side. If at any point one set of footprints vanishes (those times when we feel alone, uncertain, and troubled on our path), God promises us that He is with us. In our times of trouble, when we feel like we no longer have the strength to carry on, God will lift us higher and carry us forward—leaving His footprints beneath us on the path. His love for us will prevail. God has never and will never abandon us. God's mercy is always granted unto us all.

God isn't asking you to figure it out. He's asking you to trust that He already has.

The following poem was written by James, a young boy with auditory processing disorder.

Deus Fortitudo Mea
In the mirror, I looked to see a reflection that should
be of me.
Yet, a stranger's face now appears, changed by life and
worn by tears;
tested by loss, but sustained by hope, that God would
enable me to cope.
As I lifted him up and I sat by her bed, clinging to
every word that was said;
refusing to even hint at goodbye, for fear that the
utterance would make me cry;

praying that God would change His plan, And I could
put off becoming a man.
I asked for mercy, so they could cease suffering in
pain and rest in peace.
And the crosses I bore grew heavier still as I stood by
their graves to do God's will;
Bowing my head with each shovel of dirt, hiding my
face from disclosing the hurt.
Then slowly, I turned and walked away to quietly sit
alone and pray;
Thinking of the words I wrote long ago, *Deus fortitudo
mea;* my motto.
God is my strength, upon whom I lean; now, it all
made sense; the reflection I'd seen!
The boy I was had been challenged and tried, yet, God
was there, my light and guide.
He knew that the crosses were ones I could bear,
I'd answered His call, and He'd answered my prayer.

If you think about it, God has answered all your prayers. He just answers in one of three ways: "Yes," "Not yet," or "I have something better for you."

Amid whatever disappointments, challenges, trials, and sorrows you encounter today, step back, take a breath, say a prayer, and remember how much God loves you. Be at peace. Because in the end, everything will be okay.

Being Specific in Prayer

Years ago, a horrible hurricane came through where my mother lived in Orange, Texas. It was a category 4 hurricane that devastated the landscape of Texas and Louisiana. It caused catastrophic flooding that rivaled Hurricane Katrina in many ways. My mother lived in an area that had to be evacuated. Well, she refused. She wouldn't evacuate.

One of the things you need to know about where my mother lived is that it was on a golf course. In her backyard stood two of the most gigantic pine trees I've ever seen. They were by far the tallest trees in the entire neighborhood. If you've ever been to Southeast Texas, you know the region has enormous pine trees. The trees just tower over cities.

The hurricane grew worse, and finally, my mother agreed to evacuate. I called to check on her, and she sounded worried. I said, "Mother, what's wrong?"

She said, "Well, something I've never told you. You know those two pine trees in our backyard?"

I said, "Yeah."

She said, "You know they're the tallest in our neighborhood."

I said, "Yeah, I'm aware."

She said, "What I never told you is that I have been praying daily for God to take those trees down. They were too big and blocked sight of the house. As a widow, I didn't want someone to take advantage of me, but I didn't have the money to have them taken down."

I said, "Mother, you know God always answers prayers."

She said, "Yes, Jimmy, I know God answers prayers. I'm not concerned about that. What I'm concerned about is that I wasn't specific in my prayer. I didn't tell God in what direction I wanted the trees to be taken down."

When I showed up at the house after the hurricane passed, I realized why my mother had been concerned. Her prayers had been answered.

When I called her, she asked me about the trees. I told her, "Both trees are down."

She said, "Yes, but where?"

I told her, "One on top of our neighbors' house behind us and one on top of the neighbors' garage to the right of us."

She responded, "Well, maybe they'll start going to church then."

The whole point is that you have to be specific in your prayers. If you're going to ask God for healing and expect to heal, then be clear and specific about the healing you need. Then remain open to *receive* that healing. So many people pray for certain things, but at the same time, prepare for what will happen if those prayers aren't answered. If you're expecting the opposite result from what you are praying, how rooted in your prayer can you really be? If I'm going to pray for an incredible time in Florida while on vacation, I better be packing sunscreen, shorts, and sunglasses.

At the same time, while we must be specific in our prayer and rooted in the belief that God will answer our prayer, we must also be willing to recognize when God's will for us does not align with our prayer, or at least not for that moment. Just as we can say no to one another, God can say no to us. It's important to remember, when we pray, we only see a part of the pie. God sees us and knows all of us. He sees the bigger picture for our lives. That is why in the Lord's Prayer, we say, "Let *thy* will be done." When we pray with specificity, rooted in faith that God will hear us, while also being open enough to recognize God's will for us, that's the healthy balance. That's when our will and the will of God align. But, to discern this, we must learn to recognize what is God's voice and what is our ego's voice. As I tell people, I know when God is speaking to me. I also know when it's my own voice and not God's.

When I went through seminary, one of the things that some of the seminary formators loved to say about me was, "Oh, look at Jim. He's being a showman. Look at him. He's showing off again. There he goes entertaining."

As someone trained as an entertainer, I know when I'm entertaining, and I know when I'm not. While at seminary, "entertainer" felt like a label placed on me, meant to be derogatory or to pull me down, even at times when I knew I was, in fact, not entertaining. I knew the difference within myself. Similarly, when listening for God's voice, I've learned to discern the difference.

People have asked me, "What do I tell people if they don't know how to recognize God's voice?"

I say, "Then they're in trouble!"

The scriptures often speak of the importance of knowing God. John 17:3 says, "Now this is eternal life: that they know you, the only true God, and Jesus Christ, whom you have sent." And again, from 1 John 4:6–7, scripture says, "We are from God, and whoever knows God listens to us; but whoever is not from God does not listen to us. This is how we recognize the Spirit of truth and the spirit of falsehood. Dear friends, let us love one another, for love comes from God. Everyone who loves has been born of God and knows God." 2 Peter 3:18 says, "But grow in the grace and knowledge of our Lord and Savior Jesus Christ. To Him be glory both now and forever! Amen."

To Him be glory both now and forever . . . Amen? Amen.

Our inner relationship with God, in many ways, is a direct reflection of our outer world. How we relate to God also reflects how we relate to one another. When the mind is still, the heart is calm, and you think of God, what comes to mind? And be honest with yourself. Do we call out to God only when we need or want something? Reaching out to God as if He is an infinite vending machine in the sky? Or do we take the time and develop the relationship and understanding to also know God's will? To become aware of our own walls and barriers of our egos that prevent us from integrating God's will. Are we willing to let go of our pride and let God in? Are we willing to surrender to what we know and trust to be God's will for our lives? Will we create alongside God as an instrument for enacting and manifesting His will? Are we willing to try?

How we think about God in our private moments shares with us some of the most important insights into who we are, and of course, into our relationship with God. We discover what we care about. What we hope for, and if we're honest, what we fear.

It shows us how we love, ourselves and others, and whether we know on a deeper level that we can be more loving. More compassionate. More caring. More courageous and trusting when facing fear. More genuine in our expressions of self. More understanding of others.

Has anyone ever asked you whether the glass is half full or half empty? For the people who ask me, I say, "You're missing the point. The glass is refillable. And God is the source of infinite refills."

It's easy to complain that our glass is half empty, especially in the age of social media when everyone compares their lives based on an arbitrary number of "likes." The love of God reminds us that our glass is refillable. You sin? God forgives. You worry? God is in control. You're empty? God restores. You're alone? God is with you.

It can be challenging to remember how God replenishes us during hardships or the storms of life. Or sometimes, we create habits of negativity or complaining rather than embracing the beauty of God's creation each moment we draw breath. The truth is, it's easy to be grateful when things are going good for you. It's a lot harder to be grateful when life is punching you in the face. When you can find gratitude, no matter how good or bad things are going for you, your life gets a lot better.

I challenge everyone reading this to go twenty-four hours without complaining—not once. There are millions of people in this world who would die to trade places with you. No matter how bad you think things are or were, keep it all in perspective. When you learn to stop complaining, you make room for gratitude to blossom. Twenty-four hours, no complaining. Ready? Go . . .

Turbulence

Not too long ago, I flew from the West Coast to the East Coast on a red-eye flight. I wore my sandals, my hoodie, and my shorts, as usual, and sat in the window seat. An open seat sat between a girl in the aisle seat, who seemed to be a freshman in high school, and me. I assumed she traveled alone because no one she knew sat near her. We flew through the night, traveling over the mountainous region of the Rockies, along a route where strong turbulence usually affects the flights. That night, we happened to encounter turbulence, as I expected. The plane started rocking up and down, jolting me in my seat. As a frequent flyer, the turbulence didn't concern me much, although I became worried for her, a young girl flying on her own. I turned to check on her, and to my surprise, I found her casually playing on her cell phone. Apparently without a concern in the world. I thought, *Well, okay, she seems fine.*

The turbulence usually subsides after a few moments.

However, that night, the turbulence didn't decrease. It increased! The plane jostled up and down and side to side. It became violent. So much so that I became anxious. In fact, I pulled out my rosary and began praying. Just in case something happened, God forbid . . . I even gave myself absolution. I prayed the act of contrition, and in between prayers, I thought, *This turbulence is getting really serious.*

I looked over at the girl. There she was, still playing on her cell phone. The light from her smartphone screen bobbed up and down with the turbulence, but she seemed completely unconcerned. I didn't get it. The turbulence didn't seem to disturb her in the least. I finally broke one of my own airplane etiquette rules and tapped her on the shoulder.

Tap. Tap. Tap. (I couldn't help it. I had to know.)

I said, "Excuse me, are you okay?"

She said, "Yeah, why?"

I said, "I just didn't know if the turbulence and this bouncing around is causing you any type of concern. I see that you're not traveling with anyone."

She said, "No, I'm not concerned at all. Are you concerned?"

I brushed it off like, "No! Not at all . . . Not at all. . . ." The plane hit another pocket of turbulence, causing a sinking feeling in the pit of my stomach. I said, "Really? This doesn't bother you at all?"

She said, "No. My father is the captain of the plane."

Her words struck me.

Look at the trust she held in her parent. She knew that all would be well. We can turn that storm into the turbulence we experience in our own lives. How do we place a similar level of trust in our Heavenly Father? As people of faith who pray, who show up to church, who hopefully read scripture and profess our faith, how do we weather the storms in our own lives? In the midst of the storm, how often do we begin to panic? How often do we run in fear? Fear, remember, is not of God.

That young girl taught me something during that flight. She placed her trust unequivocally in her father. To achieve that level of T.R.U.S.T., I knew she spent *time* with her dad, built a *relationship* with her dad, and clearly *understood* her dad's skill in operating the plane. She probably understood even more than I did about what caused turbulence while we flew. She *surrendered* herself during the flight to allow her dad to do his job and keep her and us all safe. As a passenger, she *tried*. She traveled and didn't allow the turbulence to deviate her from the destination or affect her inner peace.

The turbulence bothered me. Even after thousands of logged flights over many years, my nerves still rattled and shook me to my core. I wanted to take control of the situation somehow. Even though, rationally, that made no sense. Fear gripped me as that plane jostled up and down, and my only solace became prayer. I wanted the reassurance, and ultimately, the trust in God that this young girl had in her father. The level of trust she had in her father was so strong that even in times of apparent uncertainty, her faith was rock solid—completely unshaken.

Her level of trust is what we should all seek in our relationship with the Lord. Amid our darkest hours, through life's most significant challenges of loss, heartbreak, grief, suffering, sickness, sadness, and so on, God is always there for us even when the light seems impossibly far away. He is our light and our rock. Always, always, always, the darkest hours of the night are followed by the glorious light of day. (See Renewed Thoughts in Testimonies.) Often, the light is more brilliant than we'd even expected, because God's plan for each of us is more magnificent than we could imagine. It's important to understand that sometimes God lets us hit rock bottom so that we will discover that *He is the rock* at the bottom!

When you are hanging on by a thread, make sure it's the hem of His garment.

We've all heard the phrase, "Let go and let God." In our faith, should we let go and let God? Yes, and here's why. It teaches us the importance of recognizing who is truly in charge. As human beings in a perfectly imperfect world, we realize that things don't always go our way. Or we place ourselves in situations in which we are not following the will of God. Of course, turbulence happens. Messiness happens. Sin happens. But the question becomes, "What must we do when we find ourselves misaligned from the will of God?" We must acknowledge our sin. That is why the sacrament of confession is such a blessing to us as Catholics. In confession, through reconciliation and penance, we recognize our fear and take accountability for our actions. When we acknowledge where we strayed, God hears us and embraces us with open arms.

At times, we go through periods that feel like the desert experience that God talks about in the Bible. We've all been there, at one point or another, through those moments of desolation or abandonment when we feel lost, wondering, *Where is God? Where is peace?* For some of us, many of us even, the global pandemic brought about such questions when the world cried out in anguish. But you see, God is there for us amid the suffering, just as He is in the times of rejoicing. Sometimes the most incredible moments of spiritual growth occur in the desert experience or during our darkest hours. During such trials, we are confronted with what we lack or even desperately need. Suddenly, in our raw need, we grow closer to what we yearn for, and God finds a way to guide us toward our need.

When asked about how and when to pray, Pope Francis said, "Prayer is found wherever there is a deep hunger, longing, struggle, and the question, 'Why?'" He went on to share a story, and said, "We all should be like Bartimaeus in the Gospel. This blind man in Jericho kept crying out to the Lord for help even though everyone around him told him to be quiet and not bother Jesus, who—they felt—ought not be disturbed because He was so busy. Bartimaeus did not listen and only cried out louder, with holy insistence. Jesus listened to his plea and told him his faith is what saved him." The Holy Father is basically saying, don't be afraid to ask for what you need from God in prayer.

If we profess our faith and believe in God and believe in His will for our lives, we encounter times when that faith will be tested. Such times require us to remain rooted in our faith. That's why we root ourselves in a regular practice of prayer. We build that foundation of trust with God, and our relationship becomes unshakable. Even during times of turbulence. That's why we read the scripture, so that in moments of temptation or moments of desolation and despair, we don't just scatter or succumb to fear. Instead, we gather. We come together.

It's easy to say, "Let go. Let God." But what do we really mean when we say that? Let God do what? Let God be God. God operates within His will. So even when we say, "Let go, let God," we must recognize that what may feel like a desert, or may feel as though we are lost, may actually be God guiding us through the experience needed for us to be found. We are not in control. That's one of the hardest things for people to realize. We're not, and that's okay. God never promised us everything we want. God promises us everything we need. There's a difference.

Matthew 7:7–8 reminds us, "Keep asking, and it will be given to you. Keep searching, and you will find. Keep knocking, and the door will be opened to you. For everyone who asks receives, and the one who searches finds, and to the one who knocks, the door will be opened."

Let God be God. Yes, and let us be children of God, trusting in His divine wisdom with the level of certainty of a young girl traveling on an aircraft flown by the steady hands of her father.

Bosses Day

Before becoming a traveling Missionary of Mercy, I was pastor of a parish for many years. One year, at St. Mark Catholic Church in Richmond, Kentucky, my staff purchased a gift for me on Bosses Day. They gave me a high-backed office chair. The kind of office chair that made you look like an executive. Even for those of us nonexecutives, like me. This chair was fancy. It swiveled. It leaned back and forward and went up and down. All these neat features. I was so grateful to receive such a thoughtful gift from my staff.

Just to give a little bit of preface, I'm the type of person who likes to keep the tags on things I own, you know, just in case I decide to return them. Whether I buy it or it's a gift, I just never know, so I keep the tag on.

A day or so after receiving the gift, I welcomed a couple into my office for counseling. I sat down in the chair behind my desk, and they sat across from me. We began the conversation, and suddenly the chair started to lower—by itself! I started sinking down while trying to have a serious moment with the couple. I pushed the little button under the seat and pumped myself up again. The chair raised. Then I began talking, and suddenly, down it went.

After the meeting with the couple ended, I spoke with my secretary. I said, "Something's wrong with this chair. You all gave it to me. Where did you get it?"

She said, "Office Max."

I said, "Will you please call them and tell them it's broken? It's very annoying."

She called them and later popped her head into my office to say, "Office Max wanted me to ask you, did you sit in the chair?"

I said, "Of course, I sat in the chair! How else would I know it was broken?"

She said, "Well, Office Max said, 'if you sat in the chair, then it's used, and you can't return it anymore.'"

So I continued sitting in the chair. I sat in that chair for five and a half months. Up and down, up and down—constantly! It was like a personal roller coaster behind my desk. It drove me nuts!

In May, we celebrated the last Mass of the school year. A large group attended. At the end of Mass, the children received awards, and their families and friends watched. I departed after Mass and the awards. As I walked out, I saw a young man wearing a suit and tie. He wasn't a parishioner. I just knew it. I didn't recognize him, and a shepherd knows his sheep. I approached him and said, "Hello."

The individual introduced himself and said, "I'm in town visiting."

I asked him, "What brings you into town?"

He told me, "The intentions of the Mass today were in honor

of my grandparents who died recently. My parents couldn't be here, so I'm filling in for them."

I said, "What's your name?"

He said, "My name is Mark."

I said, "Oh, cool. What do you do, Mark?"

He said, "I'm vice president of Office Max."

I responded, "You mean, like a manager of Office Max? Like, the local Office Max?"

He replied, "No, I'm vice president over Office Max within the United States. Office Max is merging with Office Depot and Staples. My job is to oversee that transition."

I lit up. An idea came to me. I said, "Would you mind coming to the office with me? Whenever someone new comes to our parish, I love to show them around the parish grounds."

He said, "Sure."

I guided him through the grounds, then detoured quickly into the parish office. I said, "Here's my secretary's office. Over here is the boardroom. Let's go into my office!"

We walked into my office, and I said, "I know this is going to sound strange, but I have this tradition. Why don't you sit in my seat, and I'll sit where the guest normally sits?"

He shook his head and said, "Oh no, Father, I couldn't do that."

I insisted. I said, "No, just sit down, Mark! Enjoy yourself!"

He sat down. While we conversed, his chair began to lower. He raised it up and continued talking with me, then it sank again. Just as I experienced for the past five months, the chair lowered over and over! Finally, Mark couldn't take it anymore. He said, "Father, what's wrong with your chair?"

I said, "It's broken!"

He said, "Where did you get it?"

I said, "Office Max, Mark! I got it at Office Max!"

Mark picked up the phone. He called Office Max of Richmond, Kentucky. He told them, "A priest will be coming into the store. Whatever this priest wants for himself, his staff, and his school, he is welcome to have it regardless of the cost. Furniture. Supplies. Anything he wants."

The fantastic thing about that story and the generosity the man showed to me and my parish is that God always provides. Not necessarily in our time. God knows what we need and when we need it. Above all, we must know and we must realize that God takes care of the big picture. We only see the situation or circumstance before us. God knows the whole picture. We must learn to recognize that God is patient. He is patient beyond measure. He sees us with the perspective of eternity, and he knows each of us by name. God waits for us. He waits for us to be ready. And if we aren't, He puts us where we need to be so that we may become prepared. He prepares us so that we may seize the opportunities that He presents for us. In God's infinite wisdom, He knows when the time is right.

Do you know the story of St. Anthony of Padua? Anthony was born into a wealthy family and raised in the church. In the year 1220, he joined the Franciscan order in the hopes of preaching to the Saracens. While traveling to begin his missionary work among the Muslims of Morocco, he fell ill and returned home. Rather than returning home as expected, Anthony's ship headed for Portugal was blown off course and forced to dock in Sicily. His ailing health continued to decline, which prevented him from pursuing his missionary work among the Saracens. While in Italy, he found a new calling and began teaching theology at Bologna, Italy, and throughout southern France. Like our Pope

Francis of today, he was admired for his simple yet profound teachings of the Catholic faith.

Anthony is one of the most well-known followers of St. Francis of Assisi. He developed a reputation throughout his life as a miracle worker. He died while traveling through Padua, where he was buried, and the town for which he received his canonized name, St. Anthony of Padua.

Saint Anthony lived in simplicity, following in the teachings of the Franciscan order, and shared his teachings in simplicity. He is quoted as saying, "The breadth of charity widens the narrow heart of the sinner." And he also said, "The life of the body is the soul; the life of the soul is Christ." His words still resound today prophetically, similar to those spoken by our current Vicar of Christ, Pope Francis.

Earlier, we discussed the importance of being specific in prayer. Are you familiar with the Unfailing Prayer to St. Anthony? Maybe this prayer will bring solace during challenging times and peace to your heart as you pray for the Lord's grace.

The prayer goes, "O Holy St. Anthony, gentlest of Saints, your love for God and charity for His creatures made you worthy when on earth to possess miraculous powers. Encouraged by this thought, I implore you to obtain for me (request). O, gentle and loving St. Anthony, whose heart was ever full of human sympathy, whisper my petition into the ears of the sweet Infant Jesus, who loved to be folded in your arms. The gratitude of my heart will ever be yours. Amen."

God always answers our prayers. His response may not always be what we expect or want, but He always grants us precisely what we need, and His mercy is always available to us all. As a reminder of the message that Pope Francis entrusted me to share with you, he wants you to know, "God is with you. God has never and will never abandon you. God's mercy is always yours."

Pappy and the Pope

I received a bottle of twenty-three-year-old Pappy Van Winkle's Family Reserve bourbon as a gift. For those who may not know bourbon, Pappy Van Winkle is a rare bourbon and often very hard to find. Kentucky is considered the birthplace of bourbon, and in Kentucky, let me just tell you, it's a big deal. And not only locally but globally, bourbon is one of the claims to fame that Kentucky is known for worldwide—bourbon, horses, and yes, of course, Kentucky Fried Chicken.

I was scheduled to fly to Rome soon thereafter for a visit with the Holy Father. My parents raised me to always bring a gift whenever you are invited to a person's home. I chose to deliver the bottle of Pappy Van Winkle as a gift for the pope because I felt it represented Kentucky. I wanted to also offer gifts to the Vatican guards and the staff who assist the Holy Father, such as his chief of security who would be hosting me on my visit. I chose to bring ten bottles of Kentucky bourbon with me to Rome. (I took a picture, it's in the Image Gallery.)

This proved to be more complicated than I thought!

First of all, TSA has rules and regulations that restrict how much alcohol can be legally packaged in your baggage and another restriction on how many bottles of alcohol may leave the country through customs. Then when you land in the country of arrival, that country has its own import regulations that limit the number of bottles allowed to cross their borders before taxes and tariffs get involved. The whole situation was above my pay grade. I had no idea! I asked friends who were more knowledgeable about the process.

I also worried that the bottles would be damaged or even stolen while in transit. The bottles were quite valuable and sought-after collectors' items. Thanks to my friends' advice, I came up with a plan to get these bottles through customs and into Rome. I had each bottle individually wrapped. Friends and I bubble-wrapped them. Then we separated the bottles between two suitcases—five inside each suitcase. I then printed a copy of the TSA rules about what was allowed and placed that on top of the wrapped bottles. I did that to let TSA know that I was aware of the rules and that I knew exactly what was in the bag.

A friend who worked at the airline (who will remain nameless) advised me that to avoid the risk of the bags being flagged, I should arrive at the airport four hours earlier than usual to check the first bag. Then, four hours later, after the staff shift change, I should check the second bag because other staff would be screening each bag, increasing my chances that at least one of the bags would make it to Rome for the pope. I did as my friend advised.

I arrived four hours early. I checked the first bag and then waited to check the second bag until one hour before I departed.

The bags made it through without a hitch.

My next period of anxiety happened when I arrived in Rome. I watched the conveyor belt at baggage claim as other bags appeared. The turnstile went around and around, and I grew concerned that Customs had flagged my bags. I stood there, a nervous wreck, silently praying, *Hail Mary, full of grace, the Lord is with thee* . . .

Then, there they were. My bags arrived. "Glory be!" (In the Image Gallery, you can see the custom luggage I travel with to make sure I never miss my bags at baggage claim.) I walked my luggage straight through Customs, again, without a hitch. I later unpacked the bottles when I made it to my room. All ten bottles of bourbon were still there and perfectly intact. Of the bottles that arrived with me, I decided to give the Pappy Van Winkle 23 to Pope Francis.

The only chance I had to give the bottle to Pope Francis would be at a gathering hosted by the Holy Father. But I'd be there along with seven hundred brother priests in the Sala Regia in the Apostolic Palace—not exactly an event where I could simply carry around a bottle of bourbon in my hands. This may sound terrible, but I brought the bottle with me hidden under my cassock. Many of my brother priests from around the world carried gifts of their own to give to Pope Francis under their cassocks. It's a whole thing that we do. I knew it could be challenging to have a personal moment with Pope Francis to present him with the gift from Kentucky. Thanks be to God; I was seated close to the front. I sat in the second row.

Meeting with the Holy Father is different today than it was

years ago. With Pope John Paul II, if you scheduled a private audience with him, you received a phone call the night before that either confirmed or disaffirmed the meeting. That was the protocol. You wouldn't know until the night before. If confirmed, you would be instructed to join the pope for Mass the next day. After which, you would go to the Apostolic Palace to meet with Pope John Paul II. The process was very informal back then. The Holy Father had no security guards in the room with him. Your name would simply be on a list, and if it was, a man would open the door for you. You would enter and meet with the Holy Father, simple as that. That was the procedure. You would have Mass with him, meet him, then go on about your day. If you met with him personally, your picture with the Holy Father would be under your pillow in an envelope for you to find when you returned to your room.

Not anymore. The world has changed. Now everyone has cameras on their cell phones. I know I'm not the only one who wants to take a selfie with the pope! Pope Francis makes an effort to connect with large groups and audiences, all in person. Three photographers travel with him, constantly snapping pictures of the encounters he shares with people. If his photographers take a photo of you, the images are available to be picked up and purchased within three hours from one of the dozens of photo kiosks in the Vatican. You can order the photos digitally or have the images printed and pick up that evening. Before COVID, the Holy Father would meet with thousands of people in St. Peter's Square each Wednesday, and his photographers would take professional photos for everyone. Post-COVID, I imagine the pope will return to meeting people by the thousands when circumstances permit.

So, after Mass, there in the Sala Regia in the Apostolic Palace, I approached Pope Francis. He greeted me, and I presented him with the bottle. The photographers started snapping pictures, and I realized the label wasn't showing. I had handed him the back of the bottle! I turned the bottle in his hand and showed him the label from Kentucky. Pope Francis graciously received the gift with a smile. He shook my hand, thanked me warmly, and acknowledged, "Oh, very good bourbon." (See our picture together in the Image Gallery.)

I shared the photo and the story on social media the next day. It blew up! I didn't expect the picture to get so much attention. Immediately, I began receiving phone calls about it. The *Herald-Leader* ran an article. Then the Associated Press ran the story. Then it was included in the monologue of *The Late Late Show with James Corden*. *Forbes*, *Esquire*, and several magazines ran a version of the story. It was everywhere!

Our world is more global today than at any other time in human history. Much more so than it was even only a handful of years ago during the time of Pope John Paul II. That is one aspect that I find so fascinating about the presence that Pope Francis embodies. He is the shepherd for the more than two billion, five hundred million Christians in the world today, and he extends welcome to *all* of humanity. He expresses great love for those marginalized within our world and those who may find themselves outside the Word of God or most in need of God's mercy and God's grace. He has a great love for the poor, the sick, and the imprisoned. He uses the tools of our time to reach the hearts and minds of people, exactly where they are in their lives. He uses the media as one such tool, amplifying the message of Christ.

Where is people's attention today? Is it on God? Is it in prayer? Is it mindfully present with those we encounter in our lives? Often, no! Our attention is on our phones. Our attention is on the media, or the TV, or the tablet, or some electronic device. Pope Francis recognizes this and meets people where they are.

Reaching out to all of humanity throughout the world, his teachings are often universal and individually insightful. He challenges people at times with his prophetic voice. He challenges us within the church, especially us as priests and within the church's hierarchy, to set aside our ideals of rank and role. Through his example, he reminds us, "Be with those for which you are called to serve."

I'm no expert, but in my opinion, Pope Francis not only talks the talk, the Holy Father also walks the walk. He is the first pope in modern-day history who doesn't live in the Apostolic Palace. He lives in a dormitory among three hundred others and eats in the cafeteria alongside his dorm mates. He regularly meets with janitors and the common folk who work throughout the Vatican. He embodies the message that he is neither above nor below any of us. He is one with us. As we are all one among the Body of Christ within the Universal Catholic Church.

Steers

I recently spoke in a town outside of Houston, Texas. While speaking there, the pastor of the parish got sick. Guess who took on the duties of the church? That's right. I stepped in to help. While serving this church and community, a young father of nine children dropped dead from a heart attack out on his farm. I didn't know the family, but there I was, ministering to them in their time of need, thanks be to God. I presided over the funeral for their family. The nine children were all farm kids. They were into the FFA club (Future Farmers of America), and all pitched in to help with the cattle and the responsibilities on the farm.

After Mass one night, I realized that two of the children had steers for sale at auction. Do you know what steers are? I don't. Well, I guess I should say I didn't because, as you'll see, I certainly learned more than I knew then. The kids had steers for sale at the livestock auction in Houston, and it was their first time going to an auction without their dad. (See the children, each with one of the steers, in the Image Gallery.)

You know what I did? I called during the auction and asked if I could bid on their steers. Someone at the auction said I could. I heard the auctioneer shouting over the loudspeaker through the phone, numbers flying all over the place. I had never bid at an auction before. You know the fast-paced auctioneer ramble that I'm talking about? He was shouting, "Bluh, blah, bluh, three to bid to buy! Would ya give three? Bluh, blah, bluh."

I didn't know what was happening. To everything I heard, I just kept responding with conviction, "I'll take it. I'll take it."

The bidding was at three dollars and fifty cents. I thought, *Three dollars and fifty cents? Are you kidding me? That steer is massive! Come on, people. Let's get this price higher. I mean, let's at least go to five dollars. Look at that thing! This is ridiculous. Are they really that cheap in Texas?* I told the person who was accepting my bids on the phone, "Go to five dollars!"

After I placed my bid, the auction became quiet. The auctioneer paused, and I didn't hear any more bids. Do you know why the crowd went silent? I didn't. The bids were per pound! The steer was twelve hundred and seventy-five pounds!

The next thing I knew, the auctioneer shouted, "Sold!"

Turned out, the auction was for not only one steer but *both* steers. I bought both the kids' steers. And it wasn't buy one get one free!

The family had seven boys and two girls. The logo on the boy's hat had a number seven with a crown, and the seven points represented each of the boys of the family. He was the second youngest of the children, and his sister was the youngest. I named the steer in the picture with the boy Cajun. The steer in the picture with the girl I named Willy.

I had never bought a steer before. I was so excited. I sent a message to Pope Francis. I wrote, "Being placed in St. Peter's Square. . . ." I sent him the pictures of the two steers and told him, "I got them both! One thousand, two hundred and seventy-five pounds each."

He wrote back, "Plenty of hamburger."

The auctioneers said they would bill me.

I didn't have that kind of money in the account, but I wasn't worried. I'm never home to get my mail anyway, so it really didn't matter. . . .

I'm joking. But I really wasn't worried. God provides. He always does.

Over two thousand pounds of frozen meat arrived at my doorstep several months later. Don't believe me? Look! (There are photos of the packaged meat overflowing in the refrigerator! See for yourself in the Image Gallery.)

It would take me a lifetime to eat that much meat. And I didn't have room to store all those packages. So what did I do? I donated it to soup kitchens and the homeless in Eastern Kentucky, one of the most impoverished areas of our nation. I didn't go into the auction knowing how God would use me when I felt that familiar tug at my heart and decided to bid on the children's steers. But because of the willingness to follow that call, thousands of meals were provided to those most in need. For those truly in need, even a single meal can make all the difference between life and death.

Have you ever looked at your life, noticed how truly blessed you are, and asked, *God, why do you continue to bless me?* If you have, then you probably know His answer: *So you can continue to be a blessing to the people around you.*

Stewardship

Merriam-Webster defines stewardship as: "the conducting, supervising, or managing of something; *especially*: the careful and responsible management of something entrusted to one's care."

Sometimes, people fail to recognize the difference between stewardship and ownership. A large group of individuals believe "this car is *my* car" or "this pew is *my* pew" or "these clothes are *my* clothes" or "this church is *my* church." Mine, mine, mine. As if they have control over it. Stewardship, however, believes, "everything I have is God's." Stewardship says, "It was given to me by God, and it freely goes back to God."

I often tell people, whether I am speaking in a church or in a business, "All this could be taken away without a moment's notice. A storm could come by and wash it all away." I say this because I've seen it happen! As such, I've based the whole premise of my life on giving and receiving. I've learned that we make a living by what we get; we make a life by what we give. Stewardship is the act of organizing each of our lives so that God can use us. So that God can spend us. It goes back to the idea that no one can become poor by giving. That is why I do random acts of kindness. God proves to me, over and over, that He provides the bounty. In return, He gives the goodness that we seek. (In Testimonies, see Paying It Forward Above 30,000 Feet.)

As a priest, as a Missionary of Mercy, as a Catholic, as a human being, I've learned that a belief system, or a religion, that gives nothing, costs nothing, suffers nothing, is worth nothing. That's because it's not so much about how much we give but how much love we put into giving. The only thing we take with us when we die is what we have given away. I think this quote from American political scientist Kalu Ndukwe Kalu sums it up when he said, "The things you do for yourself are gone when you are gone, but the things you do for others remain as your legacy."

Because I approach life in this way, some of my behavior gets raised eyebrows when visiting parishes for my speaking events. For those who have attended one of my talks, you may have seen me do this. Sometimes I will ask questions and call on people in attendance. When they get the question right, I'll look around the church and give away a potted plant as a prize. Almost always, someone from the church is bothered when I give away those plants. A $6.95 plant. Often, they purchased the plant or prepared the arrangement for the day and felt some sense of ownership about the plant.

I gave the plant away—so what? I'll get you a new one. People, it's a matter of perspective. We've got to look at the bigger picture. For example, when a young kid stands up in front of the entire parish and has the guts to speak up and answer a question correctly. That takes courage! That's an act of faith! Rather than ending the encounter there, which would be an unmemorable experience, I often invite the kid forward and give away a random item. Yes, we could look at the plant and the expense someone paid to display the plant. But look at the kid's joy! When a young child receives a gift of a $6.95 plant in front of the entire parish, in church, that becomes an experience the child will remember for years. That child will share the story with friends and family, and when that child sees another plant like the one given, who do you think will remember that moment? That kid. That kid will remember a moment of courage, faith, and rejoicing. Now let me ask you, what is more valuable? The $6.95 potted plant for display, or the moment of giving and receiving that the child will never forget? (In Testimonies, see Flowers and Whatnots.)

In basic form, such moments of giving and receiving are examples of terminology that Pope Francis defines as "New Evangelism." In other words, it is a creative way, a new way, of how to evangelize by connecting with the individual on their level. Guess what? I didn't have to quote scripture to that kid. I didn't have to teach him from a textbook about Jesus. I showed him through a plant. That doesn't for a moment mean that the textbook and the theology lessons are wrong. I'm not saying that. I'm saying it's a different form of teaching and spreading the message of Jesus Christ. "New Evangelization" is an out-of-the-box way and what Pope Francis calls us to do. To meet people where they're at in their lives. As the Holy Father, on March 28, 2013, called on the world's priests and said, "Stay close to the vulnerable, the marginalized, and to be shepherds living with the smell of the sheep. This is what I'm asking you." He said with emphasis looking up from a prepared text, "Be shepherds with the smell of sheep." I understand his words to mean for us to connect with people—all people! To relate with people. To welcome people. That's what we are called to do not only as priests but as the body of Christ, as human beings. To recognize our oneness in the eyes of God.

Giving and receiving, reciprocally, not transactionally. Giving is an expression of love and an expression of ourselves. That is why we give, not because we expect something in exchange. When we give of ourselves, our talents, our gifts, our resources, and our presence, without an expectation of, "What am I going to get in return?," we acknowledge our stewardship of the life and blessings given to us by the Lord. When we give based on the idea of ownership and possession, we give transactionally. My brothers and sisters, let me ask you this. If you're giving only based on what you expect to get in return, are you really even giving? Or are you really just coming up with a roundabout way to get something you want for yourself?

When it comes to giving and receiving, our authentic selves are the greatest gift we can give one another. And get this, to receive and be received with unconditional love when sharing our authentic selves is also the greatest form of receiving. Such giving and receiving is akin to the same unconditional love that Jesus has for us all, as children of God. As Catholics and as the living Body of Christ, that is how we are called to relate with one another.

10 Items, or Less

What does the voice of God sound like in your life? The voice of God speaks to me as a feeling. I get a sense that something needs to be enacted immediately in a situation. At times, it can be challenging to decipher, *Is this God speaking, or is this me?* With practice, over and over, you come to know. We learn to separate what comes from our own egos or agendas, from what aligns with our innermost truth and the voice of God. But each person must test that for themselves.

That's where the formula comes in—T.R.U.S.T.

To know God's voice takes time. It takes forming a relationship with God. It takes an understanding of what is God's voice and what is our own voice. When we recognize God's voice, it requires surrender. Then it is up to us to take the final and often hardest step, to try.

Often, life gets messy. The voice of God can sound muddled when we're in the messiness, and usually, it's messiness of our own making. That's why I share how important it is to spend time with God, especially time in quiet. Some of us have no trouble talking to God, or even at God, but how often do we really sit in silence and listen in return. When we become quiet and actually listen, the muddled voice becomes clear, like muddy waters that calm and settle after being disturbed.

When I hear the voice of God, often manifested as a feeling, my focus is on reacting immediately and spontaneously. I don't hesitate. I just act. For example, while traveling recently, I stopped in a grocery store to pick up a few items. I don't know if your local grocery store has an express line. This one did. I was allowed ten items in this grocery store express line. I waited my turn in line then placed my items on the checkout counter to be scanned. I heard someone behind me count aloud. They said, "Nine. Ten. Eleven. Twelve. Thirteen."

This was during the time of COVID, mind you. I thought people were supposed to give me space! Apparently, this person was not in the mood to mind their own business. I had my mask on, and I turned slowly toward the person, not really wanting to make eye contact with whoever was counting and obviously upset with me. I looked back to my items, and I kept hearing, "Nine. Ten. Eleven. Twelve. Thirteen." They finally said, "This is the express. Ten items or less."

I kept my eyes on my items as the cashier continued scanning them. I thought to myself, *I know he's not talking to* me. Really, I thought I was following the rules. I had a case of Propel water, which was twelve bottles. I considered that one item. Liquid! I also had four Hershey bars. That was one item—candy. Then I had Right Guard, Pepcid, and a couple of other items—toiletries. That was another of my items. The way I counted, I had six items!

The man had a fit. He was not happy with me. The lady who scanned my items looked at me and said, "You know, sir, this is the ten items or less express?"

I said, "I know. I have six items. I don't know why everyone is all upset."

I paid for my items and picked up my bag. The guy stepped forward to scan his items, huffing and puffing, having a fit. Because I was in the ten items or less express line with what he considered to be *thirteen* items. I looked at his items on the checkout counter . . . it seemed more than mine!

Then there it was. That feeling. It tugged at my heart. I knew it to be the voice of God, calling me to meet that man with kindness wherever he was at in his life that day. When the cashier finished scanning his thirty-seven items, I took out my credit card and paid for his groceries. He looked at me and said, "What are you doing?"

I said, "I'm buying your groceries."

He said, "Who are you?"

I said, "Apparently, someone with a little bit more joy than *you*."

Then, tears filled his eyes, and he began to cry.

He shared with me that his wife of fifty-three years had died the preceding week, that today was his first time doing the shopping since she died. After we stepped away from the checkout line, we talked. He wasn't Catholic. But you see, that didn't matter. I granted him mercy at a time when he needed it most and it touched his heart. I invited him to the 60 Minutes for Jesus event. He accepted the invitation and was welcomed at the mission the next day. It's about meeting people where they are, in what they're going through, with mercy and kindness. I find that when people are genuinely in need, they will respond in kind when invited to. (See Always Take Time in the Testimonies section.)

Yes, it's good, and it's obligatory as a Catholic, to attend Mass every Sunday. It's essential to receive the Eucharist. But there's more to being a Catholic and a Christian than just attending Mass or church. For those of you who think that just going to Mass on the weekend will get you into heaven, you're going to be sitting in the smoking section for eternity! It may sound funny, but it's true. It's better to know Jesus before you meet Him . . . stop, drop, and roll doesn't work in hell. Seriously though, you can't attend church one day each week, acting holy and pious, and then go out into the world and be everything other than what you have received. Each Sunday, you receive the Word of God. You receive Jesus through the Eucharist and share in the community of one another. You are then sent forth to *be* Jesus. The Eucharist doesn't just disappear. Through the Blessed Sacrament, Jesus becomes a part of you and *is* a part of you.

How many times have you encountered someone like the man at the grocery store in the ten items for less line? Or in traffic? Or maybe you've been that person at times too. Here's the thing—we all have. We're human. What church reminds us of each Sunday is that we're human, but we're all connected by the love of Christ. The challenge that remains for each of us after we leave church is: How will we become an embodiment of this love during the remaining days of the week?

Tony's

One night, I ate dinner at a restaurant called Tony's in Lexington, Kentucky. I sat, enjoying my meal when a woman and her husband who were sitting at the table next to me approached and asked, "Are you a Catholic priest?"

I nodded and said, "Yes."

The woman told me, "We used to be Catholic." She then proceeded to say, "There's just something about your presence sitting next to us that is providing me a lot of comfort."

I said, "I'm grateful to be able to do that. May I ask why?"

She said, "We're not from the area. Five years ago, on this day, our son was murdered. Every year on the anniversary, we travel and choose a restaurant that reminds us of our son."

I asked, "What made you choose this restaurant?"

She said, "It's called Tony's. Our son's name is Tony. Seeing you here, sitting next to us, is providing me a sign that our son is at peace. It's reminding me that I need to get back into the community. Where is your church?"

I told her, "I don't have a parish. I'm a traveling Papal Missionary of Mercy."

I then extended to her one of the crosses given to me by Pope Francis. She held the cross in her hand and burst into tears. Then and there, she decided to return to church and welcome God back into her life. (We took a picture together; it's in the Image Gallery.)

God constantly puts people in our lives for us to connect with. Every person reading this book right now is going through something other people don't know about. This is true of every person we encounter. That's why we are called to be the arms and ears and eyes of Jesus. We are called to reach out to those silently suffering and be a vessel for God in every moment of our day. Regardless of whether it's comfortable for us or not. How often do you encounter someone and act rudely or dismissively without considering what they may be dealing with in their private life?

Another example happened when eating dinner at an Outback Steakhouse in Charlotte, North Carolina. Something drew my eyes toward a couple sitting next to me. I glanced over, and we didn't make eye contact. I continued enjoying my meal, and then there it was again, I turned to look in their direction, and something told me to purchase their meal. So I did.

They finished their meal, and when they asked for the check, the waiter informed them that their bill had been paid. The lady busted down, crying. I mean, she really let her tears flow. I felt so moved by this woman's reaction. I walked over and introduced myself to try to bring her some comfort. She later shared with me that she had just left the hospital after undergoing weeks of daily radiation treatment for ovarian cancer. That meal was her and her husband's first meal together outside of the hospital.

She said, "Here I was carrying this cross, and then the waiter tells us our meal's free and already paid for. It's like an affirmation from God." She began crying again while also smiling, and she said, "Like, He's telling me it's going to be okay. That I'm going to make it through. It's like a rebirth." (Our picture together is in the Image Gallery.)

You see, all of us are called. All of us are chosen. All of us have gifts to give. It is up to us whether we listen to God's call. We all feel that nudging impulse to do what we know to be right and just and kind. That truth already lives within you. And within me too. It lives within all of us as humans. It's about trusting what lies deep within you and choosing to act. Paying it forward by purchasing a meal is a small gesture in the grand scheme of things, but in the eyes of God, it could mean *everything* to another.

We won't always know how God is using us in the lives of others, but the question is, Will we make ourselves available to acknowledge that impulse, and will we act upon it? Will we trust God's will to be delivered through us, as messengers of that which is greater than ourselves? How would your life be different if you encountered others through the eyes, ears, and heart of Jesus? How might your life become an example that would welcome others into the love and mercy God provides for us all? Because it's important to remember, His love and mercy is not something that happens *to* us—it happens *through* us.

Ruth's Chris Steak House

Whenever I travel, people often provide me with various gift cards. I'll never forget a time I spoke in New Orleans. After a talk, I received a gift card from Ruth's Chris Steak House, which happened to once be based in New Orleans. I assumed that's why the parishioner gave it to me, as a gift to remember New Orleans by. For those who aren't familiar, Ruth's Chris is a very upscale steak house. Even though I travel often, I rarely encounter their locations. It's not like there are McDonald's on every corner.

After New Orleans, I traveled to my next speaking event in Orlando, Florida. When I arrived at my hotel in Orlando, guess what restaurant happened to be directly across the street? That's right. Ruth's Chris Steak House. What are the odds? I thought, *Hmm. This has got to be a sign. I'm going to have dinner there tonight. Might as well.*

I had dinner there on a Sunday, the night before a talk was scheduled to start the following evening. When I sat down at a table, I looked at the menu and thought, *Oh my gosh, look at the prices . . . I don't even know how much this gift card is for.* You know that feeling?

Then I looked up from the menu and noticed a woman who sat with a young boy I assumed was her son. Shortly after that, she stood up, and it became clear to me that she had suffered a stroke, even at her young age. Half of her body was paralyzed, but she made every effort to stand and walk on her own. She walked with a cane, not in a wheelchair, and through sheer effort and will, she walked. Her fortitude and perseverance moved me.

Then, there it was again, that voice. It said, *What are you doing? Pay for this woman's meal.* Look *at what she's been through.* Look *how much she has achieved.* Even though I had no idea of what her internal struggles must have been, it was clear that she was persevering with grace.

I didn't hesitate. I listened to that voice and made a beeline to the cashier. I gave the cashier my card and said, "I not only want to buy this woman's meal, but I also want to purchase a one-hundred-dollar gift card for her."

On her way out, I stopped her. I introduced myself to her and her son and said, "Hi, my name is Father Jim. I know I'm a stranger. I'm a Catholic priest and a Missionary of Mercy. It is obvious that you have been through a rough patch in your life. I don't know what that was, but it looks like you're making progress. I just felt called to give you this gift card so that upon your next achievement, you can come out with your son to celebrate."

Then I never saw her again.

I shared that story of my encounter with the woman in my talk the next night. One of the unique aspects of traveling is connecting with the locals wherever I go. The people who attended the talk knew there was a Ruth's Chris Steak House in their town, so sharing that experience helps me connect with them.

What people probably don't know about me is that before presentations, I get incredibly nervous. Usually, I find a back room where I can sequester myself. Someplace where I won't have any contact with people so that I can be alone and prepare myself. That's just something I need to do. I know myself. I've got to get myself focused. I know that if I don't take that private time for myself that I'd be running around like a chicken with its head cut off, nervously gabbing to everyone in the audience.

While I was in a room, centering myself for the second night of the talk in Orlando, someone knocked on the door. I didn't answer, then there it came again.

Knock knock.

Not wanting to be disturbed, I didn't say anything in response. I thought, *Nope. Not answering. . . .*

However, sometimes God has something greater planned.

The door opened! Two gentlemen in suits entered. They said, "Father Jim, we were knocking."

Trying to avoid small talk, I said, "Oh, hello . . ."

They said, "We were at your talk last night. We were so moved by the story of the woman at Ruth's Chris Steak House," and they continued, "What you may not know is that Ruth's Chris Steak House used to be headquartered in New Orleans."

I said, "Actually, I just came from speaking there and heard about that."

They said, "What you probably don't know is that the head-quarters was moved from New Orleans to Orlando after Hurricane Katrina. I'm the CEO, and this is our CFO. We happened to be at your talk last night because this is our parish. We want to thank you for the act of generosity you gave that woman. Your story inspired us to donate five thousand dollars of gift cards for you to give out to people as you travel throughout the country."

Do you see? When we allow God to use us, He will!

We give, and we receive. When we hear the call of God and choose to act, God, in turn, hears us. God sees us and responds in kind. He moves through us and through our lives in ways far beyond anything we could imagine. And get this, it's not about the money. It's about the intention behind your action. It's about the love that you give. Love is the language of God, embodied and made manifest in the life and example of Jesus Christ. It was for His love of humanity that He gave His life. For us. Not for Himself, but for *all* of us.

In scripture, Luke 10:33–35 shares a story of giving that says, "But a Samaritan, as he traveled, came where the man was; and when he saw him, he took pity on him. He went to him and bandaged his wounds, pouring on oil and wine. Then he put the man on his own donkey, brought him to an inn, and took care of him. The next day he took out two denarii and gave them to the innkeeper. 'Look after him,' he said, 'and when I return, I will reimburse you for any extra expense you may have.'"

Then, Luke 10:36–37 poses the question, "Which of these three do you think was a neighbor to the man who fell into the hands of robbers?" The expert in the law replied, "The one who had mercy on him." Jesus told him, "Go and do likewise."

When we give of ourselves, our gifts, our efforts, and our talents with love, God meets our action with an equal or greater reaction, every time.

Super Bowl

I flew from Atlanta to New Orleans with three friends to attend the Super Bowl for my thirtieth birthday. I was so excited. The Super Bowl has always been held on or around my birthday. I was thrilled to attend to celebrate my birthday. My friends flew in coach, and the airline upgraded me to first class. I still remember I sat in row 3C, in an aisle seat. While boarding the airplane, I cheered and shouted, "Woo-hoo! It's my thirtieth birthday!" I was making a scene and having a ball. Just loving life. (Just so you know, I've never done drugs, and I don't drink. So I wasn't under the influence.) I was just excited for my thirtieth birthday, and I was living my best life that day.

A young man who appeared to be a college-aged student sat next to me, across the aisle. An older man sat next to him, who I assumed to be his father. The kid turned to me and said, "Excuse me. Are you going to the game?"

I said, "Yeah, I'm going to the game. Do you know why?"

He said, "Yeah. Woo-hoo! It's your thirtieth birthday."

I asked, "How do you know that?"

He replied, "*Everyone* knows it. You've been screaming it since we got on the plane." He then looked at me and asked, "What kind of work do you do?"

I said, "It's none of your business."

Remember, once I tell someone I'm a priest, especially on an airplane, people immediately begin to act differently . . . so I didn't bring it up.

I said, "What do you do?"

He said, "I'm in college." He then pointed to his father and said, "My dad is vice president of a chemical company called DuPont."

I asked him, "Do you go to church?"

He said, "Excuse me?"

I asked again, enunciating, "Do. You. Go. To church?"

He responded, "Oh no. We don't go to church. We're Catholic."

In a thunderous voice, I said, "What?"

He said, "Yeah. Our family stopped going to church because my dad got in an argument with the priest."

In an even louder voice, I nearly shouted, "Are you telling me that you, and your father, and your family, gave up the sacraments? Gave up the Eucharist? Gave up *your* faith and the traditions of the Church because your dad had a disagreement with the priest. Are you telling me that is how shallow your faith is?"

The man who sat in front of me, a three-hundred-and-fifty-pound African American football player for the Miami Dolphins, turned around in his seat and said, "Preach it, brother! Preach it!"

I looked to the boy and said, "Are you serious?"

The boy looked at his dad, and the dad looked at the boy. The boy then pulled a ten-dollar bill from his wallet, turned to his dad, and said, "You won. He's a Baptist preacher."

I said, "I ain't no Baptist preacher. I'm a Roman Catholic priest, and when we land in New Orleans, you and your father are going to get yourselves to confession. You're going to get absolution. And you're going to go back to church."

Every year, for twenty-two years, I have received a card on my birthday from that family. The father is now on the Diocesan Finance Council in Delaware. The son is now a Catholic campus minister at a university. As remarkable as that may be, what I find even more unique is that on February 4, 2017, who walked through the door at St. Mary Catholic Church in Orange, Texas, for my mother's funeral? The son and the father. Twenty years after our encounter on the airplane, and the first and only time I have seen them since.

We never know what God has planned for us or how our lives will unfold within God's timeline. I happened to be on a flight, and a moment presented itself where I could minister to them when they were in need. Then, twenty-some years later, at a time when I was most in need, they, in turn, were there and ministered to me. We are all connected through God—God's timeline.

The Price Is Right

I once traveled to Los Angeles, California, with my staff at the time, the church secretary, the director of Faith Formation, and the head of Campus Ministry from St. Mark Catholic Church of Richmond, Kentucky. We were there to attend a conference. When we arrived in California, I said to my staff, "The only thing I ask of you while we're here is that we eat together each night, and in return, on the final day, whatever activity you all would like to do, I'll do it with you."

They agreed, and we ate together each night. On the night before our last day, I asked them, "What would you all like to do tomorrow?"

They grew quiet and looked at one another as if hoping someone else would speak up. Like no one wanted to break the news to me for fear I'd turn it down.

I said, "What? Remember, I promised that I said I would do whatever it is you all want to do."

One of them said, "Well, Father Jim, we want to audition for a game show."

Another of my staff said, "We're here in Los Angeles, and Studio City isn't far away. Let's audition and see if we can get on a game show."

I said, "A game show? All right, let's do it."

Going into it, they knew I'm not a morning person. I'm not. Eight a.m. might as well be the crack of dawn for me. They knew this and said, "The catch is, we need to be there on the studio lot at three thirty a.m."

I said, "Three thirty in the morning. Are you crazy?"

I relented and kept my word. I would do whatever they wanted to do. I just didn't expect that whatever they came up with would drag me out of bed so early! The other issue was, what do you wear to a game show? I didn't have a clue. I had never been to a game show. Not knowing any different, I decided I would wear my clerical collar and suit, or my blacks, as I call it. It felt like I had barely closed my eyes when the alarm went off, and then there we were at 3:30 a.m., leaving the hotel. We arrived at the contestant parking lot for *The Price Is Right* around 3:50 a.m. We were herded into a line where some show hand gave me a number, something like audience member 342. No exaggeration, I asked all the people in line around me, "What is wrong with you people? Why are you here so early? Do you all not have lives? What on earth are you *doing* here?"

While in line, the show producers seemed to cull the herd and weed people out along the way. I don't know if you've ever been to a game show, but while you're standing in line for hours, they ask for your Social Security number and your tax information just in case you win a prize. They also do this to disqualify people before letting people into the audience. It's crazy. The final thing they do for *The Price Is Right* is the producer of the show divides everyone in the line into small groups, groups of five, where they interview people. That's how they select who will be on the show. It's preselected. The entire interview only consisted of one question for each person (I can't for the life of me remember what I was asked). And the process may have lasted thirty seconds for our whole group.

They chose our group to be audience members, and we walked into the studio. When I saw the lights and ushers were guiding us to our seats, I froze. I kid you not. The terror of God came upon me. I stopped midstride because I realized this was going to be on national TV. I pulled my staff to the side and gathered them in a little circle in the corner of the studio and clarified, "Whatever we do, we need to realize that we are representing the Catholic Church. Another thing we need to realize . . . Bishop doesn't know we're here."

They all understood how serious I was. I said, "If your name gets called down to contestants' row, you don't scream, you don't jump up, you simply raise your hand calmly. You walk down the aisle. You don't scream into the microphone. Just make your bid like a normal, sane person. That's it. And why don't we do all of this? Because we're representing the Church, and we don't want people to think we're crazy."

The staff from St. Mark's all agreed to the guidelines. We broke from our little powwow, walked into the studio, and took our seats. Easy-peasy. If you've never been to a game show in person, being in the audience was a high-energy experience. Music blasted through speakers to liven up the crowd. When the announcer shouted for everyone to cheer, the crowd erupted with excitement. I had never experienced such a frenzy. Soon enough, the first three contestants were called. The contestants guessed prices, and if they answered correctly, they played another game or spun the wheel. When the show went to a commercial break, the host, Drew Carey, entertained the audience with jokes while waiting for the break to end. One of the producers yelled out, counting down the time until the cameras turned on again, "One minute! Thirty seconds . . . Fifteen seconds . . ."

About ten seconds before going live, one of the show staff ran onto the stage and whispered in Drew Carey's ear. Drew smirked, and I heard him say, "Wow, we've never had one of those on the show, have we?"

"Three seconds! Two! One!"

Suddenly, a boom microphone and a crane camera dropped in front of our row. Then I heard the voice say, "Father Jim Sichko, come on down! You're the next contestant on *The Price Is Right.*"

Oh my gosh, I jumped up out of my seat. I screamed. I pushed my secretary over, and she fell into the aisle. I rushed to pick her up but instead stepped over her because I was too busy running up and down the aisle, slapping people's hands. People were pointing for me to go down to Contestants' Row.

Let me tell you something. I never, ever, ever chewed gum . . . until that day. There I was, smacking on my gum, wearing my collar. Drew Carey asked me, "Father, where are you from?"

I screamed out, "Lexington, Kentucky! Woo!"

On behalf of all Catholics everywhere, let me just say, I apologize for the embarrassing spectacle that I was that day. My goodness. And here's the thing, I won! I guessed the number then went up on stage. I played a game, and I won! I won the watch that I still wear on my wrist to this day and several other prizes.

You may not know this about *The Price Is Right*, but they give you the date in advance of when the episode will air, usually weeks away. Going to the game show was a great experience. Then we flew home. After that, I forgot that the show would come out on national TV weeks later. The day the show was scheduled to air, I woke up, bolted upright in my bed because I realized I never told the bishop. I immediately opened my computer and emailed the bishop. I thought, *The bishop's busy, right? He's busy. He doesn't have time to respond to emails. Maybe he won't get around to seeing my email today. I'll just let him know.*

I emailed him, and this is verbatim what I wrote. I said, "Dear Bishop, whatever you do today, don't watch *The Price Is Right*." That's all I said. Then I signed it, "Sincerely yours in Christ, Father Jim."

Two minutes after I sent the email—*ding*! I received an email back from the bishop.

He wrote, "Father Jim, are you telling me what I think you're telling me? Sincerely yours, Bishop."

I wrote back, "Bishop, I don't know what you think I'm telling you, but just don't watch *The Price Is Right* today."

The whole point of the story is, I can't ask my staff to do things if I'm not willing to do them myself. You can't ask your flock to follow the commandments, go to confession, or stand up for the marginalized if you aren't willing to do it yourself. Whether we know it or not, subliminally, it sends a contrary message. People are not stupid. If you don't love what you do, it shows. The same holds true about your beliefs. If you don't believe in what you're professing, it shows. We can all talk a big game until we're put on the spot. When the boom microphone drops and the crane camera light turns on, how closely are we practicing what we preach?

In what areas of your life are you professing to walk the walk, but deep down, you may only be talking the talk? That experience on the game show caused me to really take a look at myself. In moments like that, sometimes your true self comes out.

Here I told my staff, "You don't behave this way or that way. You have to be like this." And yet, when the time came, I broke all my own rules. That's why I still wear the watch from that day on my wrist. Some people wear bracelets, beads, encouraging words, or "What Would Jesus Do?" bands as gentle life reminders. I wear the watch as a constant reminder that I am called to be what I profess and practice what I preach to the best of my ability. When I fail or I goof, I take responsibility. I hold myself accountable. Even though I may fall, I pick myself up. I fall nine times; He picks me up ten. That's the beauty of a relationship with God.

Halloween

I love Halloween. One of the reasons I love Halloween is because I love giving. Each year, before the holiday, I purchase the best possible candies in the world. I don't buy the little "fun" size candies. Oh no. Not me. Whoever thought to call those little minicandies "fun" size apparently never ate candy. I get the megapacks: the six-piece Reese's Peanut Butter cups, the Snickers double packs, Hershey Bars, Crunch Bars, Twix multipacks. I buy the one-pound chocolate bars. I'm serious. I'm always so excited that I go all out!

One year, on Halloween evening, the neighborhood kids went door-to-door wearing their costumes. I watched from the window, excited, ready with my buckets of candy for the taking. They walked down the sidewalk of the street, and I thought, *Here they come! I wonder if they'll stop at my house. They know I get the best candies every year.*

Do you think they walked down the sidewalk to my porch?

No, they just kept walking past my house. Over and over, groups skipped my house while I ate the candy myself. They kept walking by without stopping, and I kept eating the candy until I realized my porch lights were off and the blinds were drawn. No wonder they weren't stopping by my house! Then, suddenly, my phone rang. I received news that one of my parishioners was in critical condition at Central Baptist Hospital. Whenever I receive such a phone call, regardless of the situation, I put on my collar, clean myself up, and hurry to be with the parishioner and their family at the hospital. That night, I anointed the person and ministered to them and their family before that person passed away.

After leaving the hospital in my collar, I realized I had eaten no dinner and only a few handfuls of candy that evening; a handful of M&M's, a Hershey Bar, and two Reese's cups. Don't get me wrong, if I could eat that for dinner, I would! I decided to stop at the Wendy's on Athens Boonesboro Road, near the interstate, on the way back to my house. I went through the drive-through and ordered a double cheeseburger, large fries, and a Diet Coke (which makes no sense whatsoever).

When I went through the drive-through, the woman leaned out of the window and said, "Real original costume."

I said, "Excuse me."

She said, "The priest outfit. That's a real original costume."

I said, "No, ma'am. This is not a costume. I'm really a priest. A Catholic priest."

She responded, "Honey, listen. I'm Catholic, and I know a priest when I see one, all right?"

She handed me the food through the window, then I drove home. As I drove, I began to wonder, *What did she mean by that? I am a priest. Why did she say that?* I wanted to know. So, the next morning, I drove back to the same Wendy's. I wore my collar again. I walked through the front door, and who did I see wiping the tables? The same woman.

Just as I began to say, "Hello . . ."

She looked up from the tables and said to me, "Wow, must have been one heck of a Halloween party. You're back!"

I didn't know what to say.

As I drove home, her words prompted me to consider my calling. Without a single shred of doubt, I know that God's calling for me is to be a priest. But still, it made me ponder, *Who are we—really?* If we are tuning in to notice God's call, are we showing up, to the best of our ability each day to answer that call, and *be* that which we are called to be? If not, then we better tune in, people! If not, let this be a wake-up call to listen for God's voice, steadily guiding you toward it with love. And if we are, let this be a reminder that it's up to us to show up to the best of our ability each day. Nike says, "Just *do* it," well, I say, "Just *be* it." Be that which we are called to be. Every now and then, it's important to check in with ourselves and ask, *Are we exemplifying our calling in life to the point where other people will notice our passion and think, "Wow, that person really embodies their calling . . ."?*

When we align our lives with purpose, God is there. In whatever we do, whether we may be a priest, a bank teller, a homemaker, or a fast-food worker. When people are truly aligned with God's purpose, it shows! Do people recognize your conviction, and do people see the image and embodiment of Jesus through you? As Catholics, we have been given the holy sacrament of the Eucharist each Sunday to help us attune with the living embodiment of Christ that He welcomes us to become. It is up to each one of us to carry that with us throughout our week and in our day-to-day interactions. God already knows your heart; do you? A meditation to reflect on: How is Christ resonating, radiating, and reflecting through you and from you, right now, and in each moment every day?

Father Harkins's Funeral

I don't understand when people question the intentions of others without first examining their own choices. For example, I heard the story of a young priest named Father Evan Patrick Harkins of St. James Parish, newly ordained in Kansas City, Missouri, who died by suicide. When I read the news, the story moved my heart with pity. Not only as a Missionary of Mercy, or as a Catholic priest, but as an individual—a fellow human being. I felt sad for him. I listened to my heart and immediately called to support his family and those most impacted by the loss of his life. I picked up the phone, called the diocese, then sent an email to the bishop of the priest's diocese. I wrote, "Dear Bishop, I left you a voice mail." (He never returned my call.) I went on to write, "My prayers and condolences regarding the sudden death of one of your young priests. As a brother priest and as a Papal Missionary of Mercy, I would be more than willing to take care of any financial expense of the funeral, should the diocese or family be in need. . . . Should you wish to verify my authenticity, you are welcome to reach out to my bishop, John Stowe."

He responded, "Father Jim, that didn't take long. The family wept when they were told of your offer and would like to accept your kindness."

After reading his response, I thought, *Why isn't the man's diocese offering to take care of the expense? Why is the opportunity for kindness and compassion coming from outside of his area?*

I acted, and I covered the expense. (See Paying Bills in Testimonies.) I trusted that God would provide. Then, as I always do, I shared the story of my encounter, knowing the haters and detractors would say, "Father Jim, why are you publicly sharing that you took care of that expense?" Such people often quote scripture to me, saying, "Matthew 6:3, When you give to the needy, do not let your left hand know what your right hand is doing, you should do it in secret."

To which I respond, "Don't worry about what I'm doing. Worry about why you're worried about what I'm doing."

The intent behind that scripture in Matthew calls us to ask ourselves, "What is the intent in our hearts?" If your intent within your heart is to show off, then yes! Shut your mouth and keep it a secret. If your intent is to use that act as a way of evangelizing the message of Jesus, then yes, proclaim it to the hilltop! Not one place in scripture did Jesus do anything in secret. In fact, He performed His healings in public so that His actions could serve as lessons to others. He performed His miracles, always, in front of others. He used His actions as an educational tool. He lived by example, letting His love radiate through the lives of those He encountered in the hopes that they carry the message in their own lives and in their own encounters among one another.

Similarly, I share these stories, situations, and experiences, hoping that others realize, "If he can do it, then so can I. I, too, can listen for the voice of God in my life and act."

It requires us only to shift from a *me* mentality to a *we* mentality. Our world is in desperate need of people to wake up. We must realize that it's not my world, it's our world, and we're all in this together. We will never change the world by going to church. We will only change the world by being the Church. The Universal Church. In the eyes of God, we are all equal as one human race. In the Lord's Prayer, we don't pray "my father," but "our father," because "I am not an only child, none of us are."

As such, when my brother or sister is in need, I, too, am in need. When giving, please remember, it is impossible to become poor by giving. God doesn't work that way. When we give, we receive, and often, when God sees our effort, He meets our act of giving ten times over, and we, in turn, receive in abundance through Christ. No one ever entered the kingdom of heaven through selfishness. And giving isn't just about money or material possessions.

The cost of being nice is zero dollars. The cost of being loyal is zero dollars. The cost of being genuine is zero dollars. It costs zero dollars to be a decent person.

Paul's Second Letter to the Corinthians 5:15 reminds us, "He died for all so that they who live might no longer live for themselves, but for Him who died and rose again on their behalf"; 1 Peter 3:8 also says, "Finally, all of you, be like-minded, be sympathetic, love one another, be compassionate and humble." Ephesians 3:17–19 says, "so that Christ may dwell in your hearts through faith. And I pray that you, being rooted and established in love, may have power, together with all the Lord's holy people, to grasp how wide and long and high and deep is the love of Christ and to know this love that surpasses knowledge—that you may be filled to the measure of all the fullness of God."

Trust me, following the impulse to act from the heart immediately does not always come without challenge. Because I don't plan these things and instead just act, I'm sure I sometimes cause my bishop and the officials in the chancery of our diocese and church more than a few gray hairs. But in just doing things immediately, you get things done!

Just do it. Or, as mentioned before, just *be* it. If I can, you most certainly can too. Act when called to act. Speak with whom you feel called to speak with. "Return," as Pope Francis says, and listen to the voice in your heart of hearts when it speaks to you.

Another example of a time when I just acted without thinking twice occurred in Eastern Kentucky. A storm hit the area and flooded the town, devastating homes and countless lives. People desperately needed essentials—food, safe-to-drink water, toilet paper, and cleaning supplies. I didn't think. I just acted. I posted the situation on social media and asked people to donate. I said, "Let's fill my garage!" I didn't have the means to host a donation drive, or the time, as often as I travel. Yet God met my effort and moved mountains to pave a path for my intentions. Not because the intentions were my own, but because the intentions were aligned with God's will and what I knew to recognize as God's voice in my life.

Someone stepped forward who knew how to put together an Amazon shopping list to accept donations. Another person on social media saw the post, reached out to me, and said, "We own a moving company. Do you need transportation for these items?"

I said, "Sure!"

Then the news heard about the donation drive and asked, "Can we help publicize this?"

"Sure!" (There's a picture in the Image Gallery.)

Community is so vital. Support is so crucial. I couldn't do what I do without the action and generosity of others. I only serve as an instrument on behalf of God. A conduit. A vessel for His will. When God moves through us, together we can move mountains, and we do! I also share acts of giving publicly because people enjoy seeing their resources and gifts put to use. That's part of the joy of giving. I find that those genuinely in need always meet the generosity with gratitude for that which they receive. They often don't care what the gift may be, but feel grateful that you thought of them, included them, and met them with kindness in their suffering.

I experienced a similar encounter with the miners of Eastern Kentucky. The coal miners performed their work then received their paychecks as usual from the mining company. However, when they went to deposit their checks, the checks bounced! I heard of their circumstance and simply posted on social media and said, "In two days, I will be in Harlan at the Catholic church. Bring your check stub to verify that you are a miner and bring one invoice in your name that needs to be paid." Most of the miners affected by the lack of payment seemed leery of religion and had never stepped foot in a Catholic church. But you see, that didn't matter. As humans, they matter.

Hundreds of miners showed up. Hundreds. The sheer number who showed up shocked me. It was a powerful sight to behold. (You can see a photo with one of the miners in the Image Gallery.)

In giving of oneself and one's resources, we not only minister to others, they in turn minister to us. For me, the encounter with the individuals felt profound. They ministered to me in ways I never imagined. The outpouring of love and gratitude they shared that day moved me. Catholic or unchurched, regardless, those people are my brothers and sisters. If I ever found myself in need in Eastern Kentucky, I guarantee you something. Those people would step up to the plate to help me in any way possible. Not necessarily through financial means, but if I traveled through Harlan County and blew a tire on the road and said to any of them, "I am stuck on the side of the road and have no idea what to do or where I'm at. Can you help me?," they would find my location and immediately help me, and most likely provide me a meal while I waited. Why? Because Jesus Christ lives within us all. We as the Catholic Church and the Catholic faith are the Universal Church, and we are all the children of God in God's eyes. That's the message Pope Francis exemplifies as our representative and the Vicar of Christ, and that's one of the many messages of Christ He challenges us to live—to love thy neighbor.

People, our world needs the love of Christ more than ever. God doesn't work through any one of us in a vacuum. He works through us all in community, in our togetherness. When we recognize and love one another as human beings first, above all, no matter one's race, religion, nationality, or creed, just as Jesus so dearly loves each and every one of us—that is the love of Christ. The love of Christ welcomes all. And no one is excluded from need. We all need at times, each in our own ways. We give when we feel called to give. We receive when we find ourselves in need. God provides—always. All of us, together, unified through the love of Christ, that is the body of Christ, alive and well, healing the brokenness in our world today. As you continue your journey of encountering beyond the pages of this book, next time you look into the eyes of a stranger or someone much closer to you, please remember, you will never look into the eyes of someone God does not love, including your own.

Afterword

BY OLIVIA NEWTON-JOHN

I met Father Sichko on a Qantas flight from Los Angeles back to Melbourne. I had just been released after a monthlong stay in the hospital at my Olivia Newton-John Centre. During the flight, Father Jim sweetly and ceremoniously handed me a beautiful silver cross. He said that the pope had given him fifty crosses personally blessed by Pope Francis himself, and he told me that he had one left, which he believed was meant for me. Father Jim explained that the pope had asked him to become one of His Holiness's emissaries, which involves traveling the globe and spreading the word of love and kindness. I was thrilled to learn that my cross was one of fifty blessed by Pope Francis and given to Father Jim to bestow to those he believed needed them.

Father Jim's kindness had incredible meaning for me at that

moment, as I had just come through a very difficult time. So, to receive this cross from Father Sichko at this moment had very deep meaning for me. We exchanged numbers when our flight landed and kept in touch by email. It turned out that Father Sichko would be returning to Melbourne the following year, so we planned to reconnect with him. He was giving a service at a church outside of Melbourne proper, so John and I left really early that Sunday morning because it was about an hour away from the city. Father Sichko offered three masses that day. We went to the first service, which was at around 7:00 a.m. because we wanted to have an opportunity to see Father Jim and talk to him in between his commitments. He is such an inspirational speaker, and the audience was enraptured by his words. At one point, there was a little child in the audience who was making a lot of noise, and instead of getting upset or angry or asking them to leave, he asked the mother to bring the child up onstage.

He proceeded to tell a story about a particular piece that he carried with him all the time, one given to him directly by Pope Francis, called a zucchetto. It was a small white hat that he said had been blessed by the pope and had even belonged to the pope. He told the story of how he received this gift from the Holy Father one early morning at the Vatican. He then placed the zucchetto on this little child's head, and the boy just stopped making noise and suddenly became extremely peaceful—it was a beautiful, magical moment.

We managed to spend a little time with Father Sichko in between his services. As you probably know now from reading his book or seeing him speak live, he is funny, charming, and has incredible faith but doesn't push it on you. He just lives it. Since then, unfortunately, we really haven't been able to see each other because of the pandemic, but he has sent me the most beautiful and thoughtful gifts and stays in touch by email and text.

I love that he sends me pictures of his beautiful dog, his bloodhound, Gracie Marie, and talks about things he is doing in his community to help during this very difficult time. I believe he is still traveling and spreading the Word, and though I am not a Catholic, I believe in God and believe in compassion, kindness, and love, which Father Sichko personifies. I am very grateful to know him and to have had this experience with him, and I will always be grateful for the beautiful cross he gave me. You just never know who you might meet on an airplane and how your paths may "cross."

Afterword

BY CHAS ALLEN

What a journey Father Jim and I have shared. We met many years ago at the Catholic high school I attended, where he was the parish minister and taught a religion class. Father Jim had a reputation as a teacher who tolerated no nonsense in his classroom, other than plenty of laughter and storytelling. He challenged his students intellectually, encouraged those who needed a nudge forward, and held his students accountable for their commitments, like turning in arduous homework assignments on time, without excuses or delay. Even though his class was considered a challenging course, it was always a highlight of the week because he enlivened the classroom with his unique sense of humor and flair for storytelling that made learning fun. (Even religion class!)

Now, he continues to share his God-given talents during the

#60MinutesforJesus events worldwide, through the written word in what is now his second published book, and with everyone he ministers to with his presence. I am grateful to share that Father Jim chose me to assist him in writing his first book, *Among Friends: Stories from the Journey*, and again with this book, Encountering God: As a Traveling Papal Missionary of Mercy. Reflecting on why Father Jim trusted me to adapt his message in written form, I feel a bit like Peter. As Father Jim describes, it's hard to say why Jesus chose Peter. Similarly, it's hard to say why Father Jim chose me. I didn't study writing at a prestigious school. I'm not the most prayerful or religious candidate he could have chosen or the most knowledgeable in the ordained experience. In fact, my writing journey began on a much different foundation. I only picked up a pen after my life hit rock bottom.

Shortly after my high school years and the tutelage of teachers like Father Jim, my life veered off course during my undergraduate years at college. I grappled with challenging life events, and rather than seeking healthy outlets to heal and grow through the pain I was experiencing, I committed a crime with three college friends. At nineteen years old, life as I knew it changed forever. I was forced to confront my pain in a jail cell and look directly into the selfish actions I knew were misaligned with my innermost truth. It was there that my eyes and my heart reopened to welcome the love of God into my life. From that humbling bedrock, I picked up a pen and began writing my first book. Eventually, the story of my lived experience was developed into a film. Now, I help other people share their stories through books and films too. By the grace of God, Father Jim has blessed me with the challenge to relate his artistry as a storyteller for God not once but twice. Like I said, it's hard to say why Father Jim chose me, but what do I know . . .

My earnest intention in translating Father Jim's message through this book is for his words to ring as true as possible to his authentic expression. His lessons of kindness, mercy, grace, trust, giving and receiving, building relationships, compassion, and unconditional love resonate with the thousands who hear him speak worldwide, just as they did with me in the classroom so many years ago. Father Jim has been a mentor and a true friend in my life, for which I am eternally grateful. Now that you've read the book, you've experienced a glimpse of Father Jim's one-of-a-kind personality and gift for storytelling. At least through the written word, for now, or maybe even at one of his speaking events, I hope his presence positively impacts your life as it has mine.

It's been a pleasure translating Father Jim's message and personality into the written word. If Father Jim's message inspires you, please, take the lessons you learned with you, out into the world, as he says. Embody the lessons that moved you. Remember the emotions that stirred and share your experience with loved ones, and share it with strangers! Take time for others and make time to be kind. Practice listening for the sound of God's voice in your own life. Soon, if you do, you'll begin to recognize that all the incredible God Moments that happen to Father Jim happen to you, too. When you notice God moving through you, inviting transformation within your heart—because you will— remember the story of Peter or maybe even the unlikely writer Father Jim chose, and act with courage because, with God, even mountains move with ease and grace.

Last, no matter what you do—do it with love. The world needs more of that.

Testimonies

The Zucchetto

God Moment: "I am in tears right now . . . as I leave this parked parking lot from night two of listening to God speak to me through you, I am truly overwhelmed! Sunday was the first time in about two months that I have attended Mass, and it was no coincidence . . . your words were exactly what I needed to hear. See, I have been feeling lately like I don't matter. I feel like I don't matter to my family; I feel like I don't matter to my friends; I feel like I don't matter to my coworkers, and I feel like I don't matter to this world. But Sunday, you, Father Jim, pulled that zucchetto out of your sleeve that was given to you by Pope Francis, and you gave me a message that day that I will never forget. You told me that I matter, I matter to God, and I am worthy of His grace and mercy. It doesn't seem like near enough, but all I can say is, "Thank you!"

The Bike (see this young boy with his bike in the Image Gallery)
God Moment: Wow, it has been a long day. My life was like a roller coaster today, up and down. However, it ends up meaningfully in a special way. I am grateful for getting the bike from Father Jim. I was also inspired and touched by his speech. Don't live in others' opinions. I thought about that for a long time because I was stuck, but I finally jumped out of my comfort zone today, and I am glad I did that! It was so good and brought some tears and happiness. There is only less than one month left in my high school life. This journey was not perfect but made me grow up a lot. Everything I got through will all become the support and gift in the future. We'll all become the most gorgeous stars. When life gives you lemons, make lemonade.

Renewed Thoughts
God Moment: "Thank you, Father Jim! I had the opportunity to attend your mission at St. Mary Magdalen Church. I was contemplating suicide. After hearing you preach about the love of Jesus for all, I no longer have that stinkin' thinkin'. Thank you for coming to Abbeville. You were just what I needed!"

Keeping the Faith
God Moment: This is my first time attending anything like this. Yes, I go to church (here and there), and yes, I've been to mandatory retreats for myself and for my children . . . this was optional, and I would've never thought to come to anything like this, but you have a gift of capturing your audience. I went to church this Sunday only because I had family in town that enjoys when we all attend Mass together . . . it brought me to you. I've been yearning for something to ignite my faith again, and I can't pinpoint

what you did and how you did it but THANK YOU. You have a true gift. I've attended both yesterday and today and plan on it tomorrow. I don't know where this will lead me and how I will continue to keep that faith "awake," but I know this is definitely a start and a reminder from God that my love for Him is still there.

Flowers and Whatnots

God Moment: I attended Mass last night at my parish, St. Mildred's, where I had the pleasure of hearing your homily. It was nice to laugh a little after a difficult week. I shared your message with three of my friends last night because I enjoyed it so much. My mother passed away at ninety-three on June 26. Her funeral was held this weekend on July 2 at St. Mildred's. Deacon Cranfill, a dear friend of the family, was the funeral celebrant. The red and yellow flowers decorating the church this weekend matched the spray on her casket and were left to decorate the church for weekend Mass.

After attending Mass on Saturday, I usually get up early and watch the Sunday Mass livestream. What you did by giving away one of the vases of flowers brought tears to my eyes . . . a lot of tears! Tears of laughter! I laughed so hard I cried! Just the type of laughter I needed so badly! As an only child, I had already lost my father many years ago, lost my sweet four-legged child of twelve years in March, and now my precious little German mother (thus the red and yellow flowers), and I have been feeling very sorry for myself. You have no idea how that moment of you handing that vase of flowers to that large family totally has made my Sunday morning! And please, please, please keep giving things away! What seemed like a comical gesture to that congregation was a huge bandage for this broken heart!

Always Take Time
God Moment: Father Jim, I wanted to thank you. I had called you only once during March when my son had committed suicide. He was only seventeen. Our conversation was what helped me most. You gave me a mental picture of Jesus embracing my son when he pulled the gun trigger, and Jesus took away all my son's pain. Thank you so much for that conversation. It helped me many times to get through.

Ask and You Shall Receive
God Moment: Two peeps showed up in my receiving line. I felt the Holy Spirit prompting me to give them one of fifty crosses blessed and personally given to me by Pope Francis. When I did, they both immediately began to weep. I did not know, but their son was the Channel 6 anchor who was killed several years prior in a car accident. His mom said to me, "I had just prayed for our son to give us a sign that he is okay." Well, ask and you shall receive!

Paying It Forward Above 30,000 Feet
God Moment: Dear Father Jim, I was the captain on your flight to Rome in April. Thank you so much for the Starbucks card. It was such a nice surprise. Your thoughtfulness was very much appreciated. Please accept this for Masses for the poor. God has blessed me in my career and family. I just retired in May. So the next time you travel to Rome I might just be riding along in coach. Thanks again!

Paying Bills
God Moment: The Lord used this man to pay my brother's

electric bill since he lost his job, his paycheck was taken back by the bank and he's owed another already, and that's just the tip of the iceberg. My brother is not a religious man and the love from people like this man, I know, is opening his eyes. I don't care if you want to get a billboard and paint your face on it and tell what you did. God used you to bless all those men and that's the point. Thank you and God bless you, sir. Also, my brother had the long, red beard. (You can see him in the Image Gallery.)

Image Gallery

Selfie with Pope Francis

Preaching to the parking lot

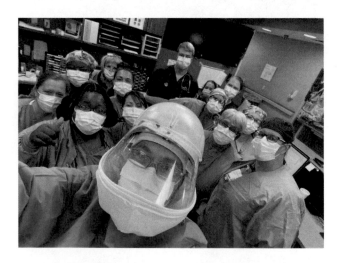

Selfie with the first responders

Picture of the Dalai Lama

Selfie with Kyle

Flowers and Whatnots

Selfie with Olivia Newton-John and John Easterling

The children and their steers, Cajun and Willy

Plenty of hamburger

Selfie with the boy who received the scholarship

The Woman in Detroit

With the Homeless

Selfie with the sanitation workers at Mom's

Selfie with Chef Giada De Laurentiis

Photos with Miss Marie's Spaghetti Sauce

More photos with Miss Marie's Spaghetti Sauce

Selfie at Tony's

Outback Steakhouse

Bourbon en route to Vatican City

Pappy and the Pope

Father Jim's luggage

Eastern Kentucky supply drive

With the Eastern Kentucky miners

We're all brothers (see Testimonies)

Kid who won the bike (see Testimonies)

About the Author

Father Jim Sichko is a priest of the diocese of Lexington, Kentucky. He was ordained to the Ministerial Priesthood of Jesus Christ on May 23, 1998. He travels throughout the United States giving missions, retreats, and days of recollection. Known for his storytelling, Father Jim weaves everyday life experiences with the rooted messages that lie within the Gospel. He is booked for speaking engagements through 2015. Each engagement lasts a minimum of three days and averages three thousand people per night. Father Jim completed his undergraduate work at New England Conservatory of Music in vocal performance and received a master of divinity degree from Sacred Heart School of Theology.

Contact Information

Father Jim Sichko

Be a part of Father Jim's daily inspirationals and testimonials:
Follow him on Instagram and Twitter @JimSichko and Facebook:
Facebook.com/jim.sichko
For more information of upcoming #60MinutesforJesus events, visit:
www.frjims.com

Miss Marie's Spaghetti Sauce

For more information on Miss Marie's Spaghetti Sauce or
where to order your own bottle, visit:
www.frjims.com

Chas Allen

Follow Chas on Instagram and Twitter @ChasAllen and
Facebook:
facebook.com/chas.allen.12
Or contact Chas by email: chasallen3@gmail.com

FATHER JIM SICHKO

FROM OPEN ROAD MEDIA

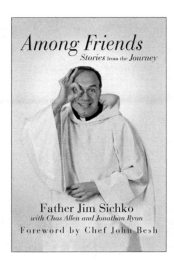

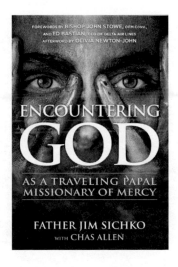

OPEN ROAD

INTEGRATED MEDIA

Find a full list of our authors and
titles at www.openroadmedia.com

FOLLOW US
@OpenRoadMedia